Seeing the World Through Women's Eyes

A collection of poems inspired by the United Nations 4th World Conference on Women - Beijing, China 1995 - compiled by the Poetry Project of the Arts Committee - Minnesota Metro Branch - Women's International League for Peace & Freedom

MINNESOTA

U.S.A.

POETRY PROJECT

19 95
BEIJING

Edited by
Naima Richmond and Marilyn M. Cuneo

Acknowledgements

Published by
> Arts Committee - Minnesota Metro Branch - Women's International League for Peace and Freedom

All rights revert to authors upon publication

Book designed and typeset by
> Artword - *Publishing & Literary Services*

Cover art by
> Naima Richmond

Photography by
> Dolores Carruth
> Marisa Cuneo-Linsly
> Carolyn Firouztash

Line art by
> Linda Thompson

Chinese paper-cut designs by
> Shen pe inong

Printed in the United States by
> Cushing-Malloy, Inc.

> ISBN 0-9655569-0-5

Table of Contents

Introduction

Meeting

PART II: RAISING OUR VOICES BOLDLY
Introduction

Woman to Woman

Girl Child

War and Peace

Race and Ethnicity

A Father Speaks

PART III: GLOBAL VOICES
Introduction

Introduction

This is a very special kind of book. It brings to public attention the voices of women from many parts of the world who chose to answer the call of the 1995 Minnesota Poetry Project to express their feelings and thoughts in poetic form. Many of these women are experienced, published poets; many others are just discovering the joys of opening themselves up to creative expression. All of them are sincere in their desire to share their experience of how the world is seen from a woman's perspective.

The Minnesota Poetry Project originated during the year-long preparations for the Fourth United Nations World Conference and Non-Governmental Organizations (NGO) Forum on Women held in Beijing and Huairou, China during August and September of 1995. The Minnesota Metro branch of the Women's International League for Peace and Freedom (WILPF), under the dynamic directorship of Carolyn Keefe, called a "Countdown to Beijing" conference in June of 1994 to begin studying the many issues scheduled to be debated at the United Nations meetings--human rights, health, violence, poverty, media, economics, education, environment, etc.--all of vital concern to women's lives. During the Countdown conference many of the participants expressed the desire to include the arts as a major form of communication between the women working on these issues and the general public. A spontaneous caucus was formed to discuss ways of incorporating a wide range of arts into the mainstream discussions. Out of that meeting the WILPF Arts Committee was born, and the Minnesota Poetry Project soon emerged as one of several major endeavors to be undertaken by the group for the Beijing conference.

We, the editors of this book--Naima Richmond and Marilyn Cuneo--have headed the project ever since. Naima, a noted Minnesota poet, is the catalyst who inspires, encourages, and nourishes people wherever she goes to make them believe that "everyone is a poet, they just don't know it." Marilyn, a former teacher of Latin American Language, Literature and Culture at the University of Minnesota, assists and supports Naima and her work. Together we have conducted poetry workshops at pre-conference meetings, on the Peace Train traveling from Helsinki to Beijing, during the NGO Forum in Huairou and at post-conference events. We distributed 10,000 bookmarks along the way requesting poems. This book is the response to that call.

Regrettably, space does not allow us to publish all of the poems we received. It is gratifying to know that so many women are giving voice to their concerns and to their creative spirits through poetry. We must not let the world ignore what they have to say.

Many contributors have expressed gratitude to us for the opportunity to let their voices be heard, but truly, we are the ones who are grateful for their enthusiastic and supportive participation. Thank you each and every one.

ENJOY!

Joan M. Drury
Minnesota - USA

Womenswords

women write poems
womenswords
small swords
a handful of quick words
stabbing the paper
between interruptions
women write poems

women write poems
words crowding their days
slipping in and out of soapy fingers
slithering down the drain
scrubbed spotless
losing their starch
pressed flat
swept under the rug
sucked up in the vacuum
tucked in grubby fingers
wordswordswords
a novel at least
women write poems

women write poems
their days bound
by incoming and outgoing words
flimsy bindings
made tough by womenswords
rosebuds sprinkled over paper
no finished gardens
a handful of petals instead
women write poems

PART I
HUAIROU AND BEIJING

INTRODUCTION

The NGO Forum in Huairou and the UN Conference in Beijing are the heart of this section. Included are:

Leaving Home   messages from women who were unable to attend

Traveling   poems written in workshops on the WILPF Peace Train as 232 women and some men from 42 countries made the trip from Helsinki to Beijing

Meeting   poems written by women at the poetry workshop we conducted in Huairou and other poems from participants at the NGO Forum

Reflecting   poems written after returning home, reflecting on the experience.

Rosemary Davis
Minnesota - USA

A Message to Beijing

May the women of the world rise up in striving to reach their own personal potentials, to meet and conquer many obstacles such as poverty and sexism, and to use collectively their social and political power to create a world that is more humane, more loving.....

Leaving Home

Helen Frost
Indiana - USA

Tomatoes

August, Fort Wayne, thunder
cracking the heat, tomatoes
drop into our hands at the slightest touch.
Cucumbers seem to appear by magic
out of the ground, like the moment you hear
an attentive silence and speak
your mind into it.

From that mind,
from that cucumber, from the rain
this thunder finally brings us,
from the silence of more than two hundred tomatoes,
the conversation that silence draws forth,
out of that dance and the music we dance to,
Ruth is leaving for China.

Ruth is leaving Fort Wayne for China,
and Mary is leaving Northfield. Gloria,
leaving Cleveland for China,
3,245 women saying goodbye in Africa,
14,833 from Europe and North America.
In Latin America and the Caribbean, 2020 women
eat and dance before flying to China.

From Asia and the Pacific,
by boat and by plane, 12,336 women,
819 more from West Asia.
33,233 women, thoughtful today,
going forth to each other.
Here we gather in love and joy
and Ruth takes us with her to China.

...   "Tomatoes" was written for a blessing ceremony for Ruth Langhenrichs before she left. ...Although I did not attend the forum, I feel that I was "a participant" through my involvement in fund-raising and communication with people who were able to attend.

Helen Frost

Terrell Lucius
Minnesota - USA

A Check List for China

> *For Jill and Rebecca on the eve of The Fourth International
> Women's Conference in Beijing, China*
>
> *(And in memory of my grandmother, Lorette Terrell, who
> traveled around the world to many places supposedly closed
> to women).*

Move strongly into the journey
making peace with the essential ache
and rapture of it;
Pack up the necessities of your heart:
the hopes, the apprehensions
Chart a geography of the unknown
with sharpened vision and indelible mind

Savor the memory-to-be that lingers
in the wash of creamy light on a temple door
or in the coy gaze of a black haired tot
who giggling peers under momma's arm;
Snap portraits through your pupil and
imprint them on your soul

Rest in each moment of the going
and let all that is shared whistle through you
like the lucid trill of a handmade flute.
Sing with joy, transcending language,
in that awesome vast chorus of women --
and as you travel be assured that
we who wait are humming too.

Vicki C. MacNabb
Minnesota - USA

Poet Dreams of Beijing

Slipping through the edge
of numbered days,
in realtime the eagles fly east,
sharp eyes cast to foreign soil
for the gathering. The familiar
touch of old soul-sisters
with new faces. Smooth, wrinkled,
open, pinched, yellow, red, brown,
white, pink, olive and Black. 40,000
variations on the theme of woman,
endlessly repeated,
endlessly new. I am
awed by the fecundity of
our species, by the labor
and fruit of our gender.

The poet sings in dreamtime,
dreaming of Beijing.
She dreams a stream of
canvas fluttering,
the wake of local experience
carried to new heights,
Midwest to Far Eastern skies.
Oceans lick their lips
with salty tongues below,
the sea snake darts to and fro
tasting for signs, the musky essence
of woman steeped like
tea in an
all-global brew.

The poet dreams, and sings stories.
Here, a story, a canvas fluttering,
a woman returns by bus, after dark,
from art classes in the city.

She is chased by a bull,
by nightmares, night fears,
by the reality of pulling a family,
a Costa Rican village,
up by the bootstraps,
up out of poverty
with a stroke of her brush.
A kiss of paint.
Doña Toribia,
how does your garden grow,
seeds planted in such desperate soil?
"I grow a feast for the valiant heart,"
says she.

The poet dreams of Chiapas,
land of hunter and hunted,
where on a silent night
humble adobe walls flickered
with the light of candles
set by cooks to honor the soul-work,
the sister-work, of a score of artists.
On a silent night, Mexican goddesses
rose in power bearing corn, bearing
the forgotten stories of origin,
of ape and cat,
the goddesses reigned over Chiapas
on a silent night, bearing milagros
for health and fortune,
bearing messages to the world.

The poet sings a song of
noble Russian women
yoked fast under the weight of history,
under eons of grey cloudy skies,
wearing thin bones and tight faces,
longing for freedom.
These Russian artists speak of
expression, a painted bird stretched
tight and sewn cruelly to canvas,
that flies, nonetheless.

A cock crows as satellites head
for the stars over Moscow,
a fairy tale lingering below.

A message of peace radiates
with poetic vision from Japan,
strong women, wives, mothers,
and daughters with glowing faces.
Self-discovery rooted in self-
portraiture. A warm mentored
teacher guides her pupils'
direct and honest eyes worldward.

And China, the poet dreams of you.
Your straight-backed artists inlaid
and layered by convention and rules.
Physician and journalist, artists-all
with the thrush, the mantis,
misty mountain peaks, dragons
of power born in perfect labor
on paper and canvas in a bare walled,
bare windowed room.
Such creations escape such austerity
under these mindful hands - a precise
balance of brush stroke,
scissors, and needle.

Ah, China, you humble
the eagles' shallow roots.
Your ancestors have forgotten
what others just begin to know.
Your rice papers and books,
porcelains and puppets, your
silkworms and Buddhas,
treasured wonders of the world,
coveted, smuggled, plundered,
guarded jealously in secret gardens
and locked fortresses.

The poet dreams.

The planet turns another revolution.
The east is before me. The east is
behind me. I swallow my tail,
talons reaching for the plum blossom
gravity of China.

Dreams merge in communion with
the Great Wall. Cheek pressed to
cold stone, molecule by molecule
the dreamer merges and passes
to the other side, barriers down,
no visa, no resistance.

Beijing -- a fat, translucent dumpling
with secret flavors.

The poet emerges,
fortune cookie in each hand,
uncertain which to choose.

She wears red to mark her arrival, to
share joy-luck desires with new sisters,
curiosity infusing their hopes,
goals, and agendas with the energies
of wisewomen and fools.

I stood by the gate in the square.
Tiananmen, I wept as the lotus women
came whispering, sighing, unfolding
their sleeves to reveal the ghosts
writhing inside. I am connected by
the very air I breathe to the
quick and the dead. I dream of silk,
black lacquer.
I dream in red.

I am filled with
revolution and wonder
even as the long arm of China
languidly reaches farther,

towards Hong Kong.

I am changed. The oceans I crossed,
I now cross anew, the planetbound
beneath me as dreamer hurtles
across the void.

I am become a red thing.
My new truths reflected in
the telling.

This poem is written in honor of Women's Art Registry of Minnesota (WARM) Beijing/NGO Conference representatives Rebecca Pavlenko and Jill Waterhouse, and in honor of the artists of WARM and their unique scroll project, **Global WARM...a message from women to the world.**

Elizabeth Erickson
Minnesota - USA

The Shore

The Women of the Earth are the Great One coming home.

They are coming home to the forest pool, the edge of the river,
the ocean shore.
They are coming home to justice for their children.

They are coming home to the voices of their elders, whispering,
"Steward the soil for seven generations down."

They are coming home to the broken and contrite hearts of this
universe, who have learned the futility of greed and the bomb.

They are coming home to the streets of their cities and villages,
walking long distances, each alone, dignified and safe,
under the night sky.

The women of the Earth are coming home to stand in the truth they
know and have known:

>The cycles of life are the crucial physics.
>Patterns move in and out of the void,
>and all this is love.

>Kindness from the hands
>discernment from the heart
>passion for the people and their places

>holy holy holy

>the men are listening
>gather and feed each other

>the Women and the Men of the Earth are
>The Great One coming home.

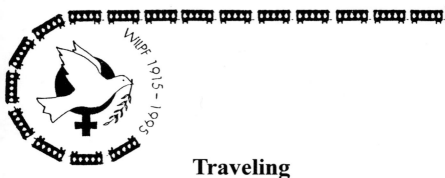

Traveling

Dedicated to the memory of Jack Wilson who died in a bus accident in the Spring of 1996 while traveling with Pennsylvania students in India. Jack accompanied his wife, Teresa, on the Peace Train en route to the UN 4th World Conference on Women and left fond memories of himself with his fellow travelers. Thank you, Jack, for sharing your friendly ways with all of us.

The Editors

John M. Wilson
Pennsylvania - USA

A Peace Train from Helsinki
(Can be sung to "Ghost Riders in the Sky")

A peace train from Helsinki went south one sunny day.
On board were lots of women, and they found to their dismay,
And a bolt of fear ran through them,
When they found some <u>men</u> on board,
Who signed up for the journey to make <u>plow shares</u> out of swords.

CHORUS: YI - PI - YI - AY -- YI - PI - YI - YO

THE PEACE TRAIN TO BEIJING

But all was not so peaceful for just a day or two.
They called each other <u>Girls</u> and <u>Boys,</u> and that was not quite true.
So they gave out gifts to everyone like pins and posters, too;
And even passed out condoms--I think we all got <u>two</u>.

The women on this peace train are not at all the same.
You can tell them by their colors, and by their different names.
They come from many countries, and it's peace, they're here to seek.
But the thing they have in common is they're not afraid to speak.

The men are quite a docile lot, at least it seems to me;
They talk among themselves so much on what they hear and see.
So when they got to Istanbul, some people thought them weird,
But they laughed because they found that Goddess <u>Sophia</u> had a <u>beard</u>!

Then there was Moldova, I thought it was quite nice.
The border guards kept coming round--I know they did it thrice.
They gathered in the railway car, and on our doors did pound.
I know nothing of their country, since we never touched the ground.

From Finland to St. Petersburg to Kiev and Bucharest,
The issues were a-flowing, so that women could be best.
But now and then within the car, you heard the music play.
The women they were"living high" before they "hit the hay."

So onward to Odessa, just to be close by the sea.
Our hotel was quite a dingy place, as rundown as could be.
The Chinese they played ping pong, I'm afraid we were the ball.
Seems they want us two days later, and it's us that has to stall.

The train rolls on across the steppe, I could not ask for more.
The sky is vast, the land is FLAT--just east of Volga's Shore.
There's sheep and horses on the plain, a village here and there,
And gardens by their little shacks well tended with much care.

Our little cabin's crowded and my clothes are on a hook.
My water bottle's ready, and I do not have to cook.
The atmosphere is cozy, and my back is not too sore,
And I'm glad I'm in a cabin that sleeps <u>two</u> instead of <u>four</u>!

Now everyone is happy, and it's issues through and through,
Around about and in-and-out, there'll never be a few.
So on we go to Beijing town with spirits high anew,
And God, <u>she's</u> in her heaven, but some <u>men</u> may be there, too.

Miriam Butterworth
Connecticut - USA

Peace Train Nightmare

Is that Tatiana at the door? Breathe deep and count to ten.
It's 4 o'clock in the morning, so it's Moldova again.

Though problems of Bulgaria may be well beyond our ken,
We know one thing: at 4 AM it's Moldova again.

There's always a new rumor, about where we'll be and when,
But at 4 o'clock each morning it's Moldova again.

One thing we have in common, be we Bahai or follower of Zen,
If it's 4 o'clock in the morning, we're in Moldova again.

I think we're getting testy. Could it be the estrogen?
No, it's just because it's 4 AM and it's Moldova again.

We think we're making progress, but no matter where we've been.
By 4 AM each morning, it's Moldova again.

We're 234 women and about a dozen men.
Can't one of us deflect our train from Moldova again?

The train passed through Moldova twice, as it traveled to and from
Ukraine to Romania. Each time all the wheels had to be changed to
conform to the differently gauged tracks--always at 4:00 am.

The Editors

Sally Shannon
Minnesota - USA

The Journey

Rumbling, crowded meeting wagons.
Bread, cheese, salty mineral water,
    lemon-filled sandwich cookies.
I never knew a sponge bath
    could feel so good!
Braving the snapping jaws to
    pass between wagons.
Two o'clock a.m. passport checks.
The train arrives at the
    station as I arrive at the
    toilet!
The train gently rocks me
    to sleep.

All of the new faces, the new
    friends, the conversations
    that have fundamentally
    changed me.
The hard questions I have
    never come face to face with.

I have learned so much about
    myself, about women, about
    the world.
And I have so many new
    questions.

How will this all come together
    for me? How will this
    all come together for
    those who I share my
    adventures and experiences
    with?

I have faithfully kept my

journal; I have captured
what I hope will be
powerful images on film;
and I have lots of
notes in my notebook.

But most important to me
        are the names of all my
        new friends, whether a
        women's health care worker
        I talked with for a few
        moments, or my dear
        friends of just three weeks;
        and the promise of
        ongoing friendships, working
        partnerships; and the
        inspiration of knowing
        that we strong and
        talented women are out
        there, working to make
        this world a better place.

Peace Train

Lofty goals
Global issues
Promising plans for action
But where is the celebration?
We women are spiritual,
        loving, compassionate beings;
        these are special gifts.
Yet we close them out as we
        strive for peace, freedom,
        economic equality.
Sometimes ugly, often
        unproductive traits take
        over--qualities favored
        by our male dominated
        world.

Even in this unique environment,
    the task is daunting.
How can we overcome?

Ali Riza Tekeloğlu
TURKEY

Barís Treni Geǵti *(Peace Train Passed By)*

Barış, herkesin özlemi; benimde özlemim,
bu, dünyâ herkese, yetecek kadar büyük.
O, trenle beride, yolculuk, etmek istedim,
sizinle, tüm insanlık, kardeşlik ve barış için.
Destekliyorum, hepinizi, cani gönülden,
ve, tüm varlığımla -
Sevgiler, saygılar, mutluluk ve başarılar.

Ali Riza Tekeloğlu
TURKEY

Peace Train Passed By
    (English translation by Zehra Avsar Keye)

Peace is everyone's desire
My desire is peace also
This world is big enough for everyone
I would like to travel with the Peace Train
With all the people who are for humanity,
    brotherhood and peace
I am supporting all of you, from the bottom of my heart
    and with all of my soul
With love, with respect, happiness and success.

Through Women's Eyes - 21

Dorothy Crabb
Minnesota - USA

Dancing Socks and Underwear

Dancing socks and underwear
Decorate our room
Past the windows birches flash
The Peace Train is our womb

We speed past back yard gardens
We hear of nuclear doom
We imagine women's lives
The Peace Train is our womb

The cities offer speeches
Fine tours, a hero's tomb
We wonder if the truth is heard
The Peace Train is our womb

When we arrive in Beijing
Reality will loom
How effective can we be?
The Peace Train <u>was</u> our womb

The Mystery Route

Shirts foretold a straight line to Beijing
Crossing borders seeking peace.
Train meanderings soon deny it.
Global women cannot buy it.
Lively talks again increase.
Now south, now north, now east, now west
We curve our way across the land
It's certain that we'll never rest
Until the Peace Train route as planned
Delivers us with peaceful singing

Maureen Morrison Long
Oregon - USA

Peace Train Challenge
(August 8, 1995, Peace Train en route on old Silk Road to Beijing)

What an odd collection this good
    Peace Train contains
While each person has strength, we
    each can be urbane.

Many are well-traveled, plus a few are
    "well-heeled,"
But money, degrees, experience have
    NO place in how we feel.

How each got aboard this train is
    a total of 232 tales;
Via 42 nations and 23 states from
    Helsinki we set sail!

Two trains, nine towns later we
    arrived in ol' Beijing
A bit tired and dirty, but at the Peace
    Tent our voices will ring.

Much talk, workshops and meetings all
    our energy have consumed.
As study, learning and fun was had
    with no schedule ever assumed.

Hang loose, adapt, be cheerful in
    whatever cause we choose
With peace and freedom foremost,
    working together in love, we can't lose!

Elizabeth Huibregtse
Colorado - USA

Unknown Friends
(Written in the night, between Romania and Bulgaria)

In the darkness, from the Peace Train
    distant spots of light,
    homes of unknown people . . .
    now we feel connected.
Does it matter?

Enclosed within, but always waving,
    First in Russia and Ukraine,
    soon Romania and Bulgaria,
    smiles and waves and then we're gone;
through Turkey and Kazakhstan, before Beijing.

        We're here with you,
        We're gone from you.
        Our eyes connected . . .
        What is your life?
        We try to know.

When we stop, we find new friends,
    Instant friends, and somehow love.
    We glimpse your past, your life today.
    How can we help but ache with you?
You're much too brave.

Perhaps we are the unknown people
    Hurrying onward to Beijing.
    Nothing left but haunting memories . . .
    Can they matter? Somehow they must,
right at this moment, and forever.

Naima Richmond
Minnesota - USA

Peace Train Riders

With much anticipation, reservations, and procrastinations
Two hundred forty-two Peace Train Riders gathered from far and near
Of this great hemisphere in Helsinki, Finland
With a strong determination to reach our destination
So onward to Beijing, China for the United Nations Fourth World
Conference on Women we go
With a sprinkling of our male supporters.

As of to date, August 13, 1995, the Peace Train
Has taken us from St. Petersburg, Ukraine, Romania and Bulgaria
Many of these places we've dreamed of
Now became a reality.

Going from country to country,
At the train stations we saw many
Hollow faces, faces which reminded me
Of the many familiar faces in my country
People who seem to feel saturated with
No hope for a better tomorrow
And like back home there is plenty
Of wealth that is apparent as we are
Shown beautiful architecture and buildings
Where we dine by dignitaries.

Yes, the hospitality showered upon us
On this great journey and the insight
That we have gained from various meetings
Are forever embedded in our hearts
But the PEACE Train has become our home
Away from home so after a stay in each
Country we long to go home
Even our PEACE Train crew is glad
To see us return from each stop we make.

We have made friends, become care-givers

And nurturers too
The bonding between the young and the old
Both learning from each others' stories told
This is not to say that there have been no
Misunderstandings on the Peace Train
But with patience, tolerance and PEACE
Being at the forefront of matters,
Issues were resolved with smooth handling.

Edith Daly
Florida - USA

Asian Eyes

Asian faces peer in at me
and I peer out at them
questioning the stereotypes in my head,
raindrops in puddles
are the only familiar sights.
In her face the same puzzled look.
What is your life like,
my sister?
Your loaf a different shape
though we must both
rise, like bread,
together from the same wheat.
We gather, from different sources,
our grain,
grown from different soil,
ground by different forces
and yet,
we bake and eat
to feed the same hunger.

Annie Wright
Rhode Island - USA

Compartment Five

Inside our snug compartment all is cozy, peaceful.

Up and down the train schisms of age, race, customs, nationality have splintered the unity of 234 women. We had hoped for unity, quiet conversations, the exhilaration in being with so many who have so much in common. Instead there are strident voices, anger, distrust from the few, which reach out to the many.

Outside the train is China, an enormous expanse of land under an enormous expanse of sky, splintered into different landscapes.

A green and gold Van Gogh scene where fields of corn, melon, cabbage and sun flowers are separated by lines of poplar trees.

Villages made of mud bricks, each compound surrounded by a mud brick wall, each village surrounded by a taller mud brick wall.

Mountains--bare brown rocks rutted like a sand hill after a rain storm. Craggy, rough, lumpy mountains with purple shadows. Rugged slopes of rust-red blown into sculptures by wind.

People make the landscapes live. A group of farmers in a compound surrounded by hay stacks spread out the harvest on the dry mud yard. A woman with a hoe alone in a big field. A man holds two long fishing poles over a muddy pool. A man with a sickle cuts green grass. Miles later another man piles hay in a wooden wagon with sides made from woven straw. His little donkey wears red tassels on his mane. Three women with white masks and colorful head scarfs of fuchsia, green and blue work on a railroad bed. A mother and her son gather herbs on the back of the trucks.

Flocks of sheep, one flock the color of the sandy soil, another, brown and black tended by shepherds in white capes. A herd of cattle rounded up by a rancher on a horse.

We four--Marisa, Marilyn, Miki, and me--have made a peace compartment in number five, our own unit. Our own kingdom.

Luna Macdonald
Montana - USA

Gobi Desert

Sparse tufts
braving dawn's pink sands

Harsh moonscapes
rising from grey stones
worn pebbles
eons of wind

Digging trenches
backs sun parched
baked dryness
where do they live?

Rust mesas
buttes soar orange
from scoured earth
geometric silhouettes

Camels
real and imagined
plod sand dunes
silk road ribbon
across the ages

Dots of adobe houses
sun flowers sparkle
lush
jewels of corn
emerald cabbages and trees
from where arises the water?

Faded distant eyes
tending sheep
folding around

tree patches
Great Wall tailings

Endless tracks

Judith M Seifker
Washington - USA

Non-Anagram

Please pass the peace
Eat all you want of ecstasy
Allocate some to all
Consume the consensus
Elevate glasses of elucidation.

Treat everyone to trust
Resist swallows of rancor
Address sustaining activity
Initiate draughts of illumination
Nurture non-violence

Cheryl Fennell
CANADA

This is a poem I wrote as we flew through 8 time zones and 1 international Date Line to be with a world of women in Beijing.

Open Skies
> *(August 26, 1995 over the North Pacific Ocean)*

Beyond time,
Above space,
We soar.
Our wings no longer weighted
Our vision straight ahead,
Our thoughts enlighten the path
And burn the skies cold haze.
What greater day we sing,
What kinder peace we bring?

Meeting

Carolyn Noble
AUSTRALIA

Pictures on Pages

I sit here in this workshop
waiting for inspiration
many pens moving to create
pictures and ideas ...all around me

Still I can't write ...though I am
thinking. I am at least sharing
the embryonic ideas that start
that movement into pictures

But just now
I am waiting to hear the ideas
that are being held on those pages

And I am excited
for, although I can't write

I can at least hear

LaVerne (Lovey) Lein
Minnesota - USA

City of Walls

We are women used to accomplishing
    together what we believe needs doing,
For ourselves, for our children, for our families,
    for our community, and for the world.
We have planned, we have prepared,
We have paid extensively to fulfill our
    commitment to work together for world peace.

And here we are, together, yet impossibly apart,
Wonderful meetings, all kept apart by walls
    which encase little areas of buildings;
Time schedules, normal for other world conferences,
Impossible because of walls
Venues a short distance apart,
    made extensive because of superfluous gates and walls.

What have these walls created for China?
What have these walls created for us?
We tire so from circumventing them all day
    long in humid, hot, drippy haze.
The extra blocks because walls were built
    fulfill their purpose of destroying ease of communication;
Tire those of us who are shorter of stamina,
    yet grandiose with wisdom.

The officials zoom out pampered
    in shiny white embassy cars,
    from inside gates holding secluded walled living quarters--
No walking for them!

The number 2 reached, cannot be crossed
    to reach the number 3 site,
    which is all within walls
    forbidding walking to number 4 site.

Maps confuse from lack of perspective,
    lack of scale to distance.
The child would draw maps this way.

We who have weathered China's non-explainable illogic
    are ready for home.
We're anxious
    for order without walls,
    for personal respect without threat,
    for state fairs without division of spaces
    into gates and high barriers.

The purpose of isolation and discomfort and inability to meet together
    dis-empowering women with needless intervention and threat
    has been accomplished.
The hotels give us no spaces to meet to learn from one another.
The people sipping drinks are questioned
    whether they're having a meeting.
The women walk and walk and walk, missing precious
    meetings spaced distances from one another.

Yet we shall meet and we shall continue our work
    in other spaces and places
    in other parts of the world,
Without the walls, without the separations, without the barriers,
    we will accomplish our work.
Love and caring move beyond all barriers and constructions.
We construct our own shared dreams and cares together,
    wherever in the world we might return to.

We are the courage!
We are the strength!
The walls will become transparent and disintegrate,
    For we know we are together now and forever.
        Forever world women are we now.

Joy Bove Lurken
Florida - USA

Beijing March 95

Why does my heart beat so strongly?
Why do tears stream down my face?
When I see women march to the drum beat.
Their faces brown, black and white.
Their eyes all shapes and colors.
Their dresses flowing rainbows.
Yet all of them carry their banner high
The words say, "No Violence" "No War"
    "Peace Now"

And now I know--It is because they ask for so little,
And yet it is our right to have it now!
    YES NOW!!

Monica Ertel
California - USA

Untitled

City of Women
- vibrant
- chaotic
- colorful
- nurturing
- powerful

All sisters in spirit
Building one global village
A city of hope

Tiananmen Square

Little china doll
Proudly holding your skirt
Mother and father capturing your image
With Chairman Mao smiling from above
Little girl - a precious gift
Unwanted and discarded by the masses

Geeta Mahajan
INDIA

Rainbow

Here in Beijing -
We, the daughters of seven continents -
Converge, merge and resonate to create
a beautiful Rainbow
like the one the Earth has never seen before.

Rainbow not just of hopes and dreams
but of resolute wills
to shine on the horizon of history
and create a world beautiful from within.

Rainbow signifying -
Sunshine and the moist at the same time
Here is the Rainbow -
of strength and kindness at the same time

Here we create an exquisite bridge, a strong bond -
to bend the unbendable -
to flex the inflexible -
and, to change the so far unchangeable.

And there !
We mend the Rainbow into a shining plough -
a powerful plough
to till the hardest of the soils
to harvest a full season
of health and happiness for all.

Here in Beijing,
we, the sisters from seven continents
resonate to create
a beautiful Rainbow
as the one the Earth has never beheld before.

Margaret Metzler
CHINA

Words - Heard at the NGO Forum, September 1995

Empowerment, mutilation...
graft, greed and proliferation
of military might and power...
hunger, death and despair...
the Media...what to wear...
the feminine and the masculine...
hierarchy-computers
CNN and Reuters...
no blackboards or chalk...
what's the right way to walk?
education for all...
the shopping mall.
Parents line up at night
so children have the right
to attend the school.
Bring back our sons!
(Being held hostage)
and every other outrage
done against women.
Treated as chattel,
bought and sold like cattle.
Married at five...
at 18 barely alive
Beaten by those
who say she belongs
    to them and they have the right.
She doesn't.
Abandoned at birth,
nothing of worth...
But one granddaughter
told how her grandfather
(having recently believed
in the One and Only
Creator of all)
commanded his daughter

NOT be drowned in the river.
"So I'm here today!"
Some girl children
are refused life beyond
      a few weeks in the womb.
      It becomes a tomb.
Compassion and love
softness, virtue, kindness,
Identity--maternity
economy...anatomy
Accessibility...Aids...youth
false and truth
War and peace
prisoner's release...
death, life, love and evil,
Strong and weak
aged and feeble...
disabled, enabled, labeled...
respect for some but not for others...
sister, grandmothers,
wives and mothers...
slavery and prostitution
legitimize as the solution...
male domination and woman's place...
anything other is just disgrace...
global needs and global issues.
Rich and poor, North and South,
Creator God, Father, Mother,
Allah, Eloahim, Sacred Other...

Words full of meaning
Still silently screaming
in the hearts of the hearers.

Jennifer Cregan
Missouri - USA

ONE Day

The voices echo
Our sisters past
Their lives, our lesson
Their words, our story

As their journey ends
Ours has just begun
Different
Yet, somehow the same

We fight our sisters' battles
As they have been fighting ours

We take a step forward
The world makes us step back
We push our way forward
And the world pushes back
We charge forward as ONE
And the world must finally listen

Julanne Sweeney
AUSTRALIA

Beijing Symphony: Evade the Truth (also known as the Dodgy)

That some may not be born equal
That to many, much is given
And little expected

That the same sun rises above us
That blood fuels every woman -
And man in lesser ways

That colour, music, dance and art
Are weapons to unite and heal -

For female genital mutilation?
For the battered Irish wife in the Tribunal?
For the Bahai flamenco dancer from Hawaii
        whose purple hair and green costume
        repeat the theme?
For the Ugandan, Algerian, Rwandan
        who bared their souls
And humbled the dominant-language
        speakers into interpreting machines?

That silence is consent in Beijing
That censorship and right to speak
Are in the too-hard composition basket

That a call to arms is resonating
That QUOTAS for women
And training for their ROLES
Are only the rehearsal

That women will be
Both Instruments and Players
        in this Orchestra.

Susan Michele Frain
Missouri - USA

Food, Glorious Food

Reflections on a workshop entitled,
"Changing the Food Aid Agenda:
Empowering Women in Crisis"

In Mozambique
There is not enough
In the U.S.
I go to Overeaters Anonymous
In Pakistan
There is one bowl a day
In the U.S.
I go on a diet
In Sierra Leone
It is taken from children
In the U.S.
I throw it away
In Rwanda
It is given to the men who do not share
In the U.S.
I always have it
Food, Glorious Food

Ruth Rasnic
ISRAEL

The Untowering of Babel

The Tower of Babel
The pinnacle of man's discord
The babbling tongues
Confused, confusing
Leading humanity
To eternal wars.

The workshop on social change
Where twenty women proved
In word and empathy
That towers can be
Brought to ground
As my sister from Nippon
Broke down in my arms
And her anguish
Pulsated through the room.

Susan Faupel
Illinois - USA

Women Unite

Thousands of women all around
Banners stretched along the ground
Feelings of love, beauty and peace abound
The power of women both old and new found.
Demanding our rights with fists we pound
To break free from chains too tightly bound
Many different voices join to make the sound
"WOMEN UNITE! CHANGE OUR WORLD AROUND!"

Marilyn M. Cuneo
Minnesota - USA

. . . . . Connecting the Dots . . . . .

On the map of the world
here I am,
a molecular dot
way up north and center,
doing my thing.

On the map of the world
there you are,
and you, and you,
and millions of you's . . . . .
dot after dot
in Asia
in Africa
in Europe
in the Americas,
here and there,
each alone, separate,
doing your thing.

On the map of the world
draw a line
connecting dot to dot,
joining the me's to the you's,
uniting us in a single image:

> all-encompassing,
> stunning in its enormity,
> its power, its relevance.

A picture of women worldwide
doing our thing:

> Making connections
> Making a difference
> Making peace . . . . .

Feride Papleka
ALBANIA

It's Raining

"Let me cry at the sea-side"
--Góngora

I bought a train:
A toy train for my son.
A train like one I couldn't buy sometime.
A train which became a sadness full mountain.
Where is the childhood of my son?

I Am All in Waiting

"Optimus Maximus"
(Epithet of Jupiter in the Roman Pantheon)

I am all in waiting.
I predict gilding of a sun over my head.
A sun as an unaltered god shaped,
I predict long trips,
Along vanished rivers' courses
That we miss, as lost amours we are longing for;
On mountains sunk to the sea,
With mythical death-rattles under water,
And silver chaplets of trees,
That undying deads remind us of;
Along forgotten paths,
That their revival from old maps dream.

Dorothy Haegele
Florida - USA

Birthing Real Humanity

Give birth in Beijing to the rapture of knowing
That hatred and shame can be shed,
That warlords and clergy have nothing to offer,
Except reason to wish you were dead.

For centuries men have been trying to prove
That male domination is right.
They ridicule sons for acknowledging hurts
Or trying to avoid a fight.

From a very young age they train them for war
And send con men into schools,
Who lie through their teeth to lure students
Into the killing pools.

Military tactics, refined with precision,
Instill confusion, hatred and fear.
If the victims come home, that comes with them.
We now have the violence here.

Only women will save them.
That's the message of many a sage.
Then let's do it. Why wait?
We are all the ideal age.

So, give birth today, in a painless way,
To the rapture of mind liberation.
To insights and genius inherent in all;
We're not on Earth for probation.

Who tells us human nature is flawed,
And gives us that bit about sinners?
In spite of the brain-washing job done on us
We humans are admirable winners.

We're here to claim what is rightfully ours,
Vast human potential for good,
Without patriarchy's distortion and lies,
Dished out as spiritual food.

Affirming the joy of nurturing life,
Men and women with genius untainted
We're human. We're fine, in spite of religion,
and none of us wants to be sainted.

We reject the sin peddlers' message of fear
and their sick obsession with sex,
so, trusting our essence - intelligent good,
we will no longer play with stacked decks.

We are doing our thing in Beijing
To take back our minds and our joy,
Strength, valor and genius are rightfully ours, -
Religious trappings a ploy.

Enough of sin, sorrow and shame!
Be gone with labeling, hatred & killing
We are human, proud of our wholeness and beauty.
Respect our acumen. Be willing.

Old patriarchs fear an awakening,
Privileged males don't know what to think.
Responsibility for their behavior
Sends them fleeing in search of a shrink.

It's okay, guys. You'll like it,
In a family of humans who care
About each other, about all people's children
And who seek to clean up the air.

No longer looking for others to punish
Or finding scapegoats to blame,
Leaves us free to develop potential
and make workable rules for the game.

Old men in long robes may warn you of hell,
Those in uniforms tell you you're doomed,
If you won't kill your brothers and sisters
To further the corporate boom.

This is a new beginning
We are giving birth today
And we'll raise up these strong, young ideas
By reclaiming humanity's way.

Julia Uleberg
Minnesota - USA

The Market Place
Huairou, China, 1995

I walk along a Chinese
      market place
    A cacophony of sounds
      and voices greet my ear.

"Over here lady.
    I give you good price
      verdy good price."

I look at women's work
    hanging in the stalls.
Beautiful hand stitched table cloths
      flutter like large flaps in the breeze
    their images transport me
      back to a
      Minnesota farm kitchen
    and the memory of a grandmother's hands
      as she stitches beautiful
        table cloths.

After she dies
    I keep one of her
    table cloths
    Threads weaving me
      to the women of my past
      a sacred gift
    I hold close to my heart.

"I give you a good price
    a verdy good price
      for friend good price"

I am back in China
    gently holding

                    threads
             weaving me to
                    other women's lives.

I will carry these
             lives back
      to Minnesota
where they will rest
      gracefully upon
             my
                    table.

Neng Magno
HONG KONG

"Third World" Women

Faces ashen by cooking
hands rough with scrubbing
breasts and bellies sagging with birthing and feeding.
Marginalized and de-valued
by *this* globalized world
of consumption and domination.

Linking arms, clasping hands
stomping feet in rhythmic precision
lives and souls connected.
Women of *our* world
asserting rights, calling for change
celebrating solidarity in diversity here and now!

Sara Yeraka
California - USA

Sitting in Tranquility

Sitting in tranquility - by lake Yanxi.
A land I never thought to visit
   if it were not for the 1995
   Beijing Women's Conference.

Sitting in tranquility - by lake Yanxi.
Enlightened my objectivity.
This led me to perceive the Chinese
   paintings with deeper understanding.

Sitting in tranquility - by lake Yanxi
Contemplating: the mist; the atmosphere; the
hills; the trees; the lake; the stillness . . . .
The soothing Chinese tune in the background.

Sitting in tranquility - by lake Yanxi.
An experience of connectedness and
   spiritual healing.
A veil removing prejudice.

Sitting in tranquility - by lake Yanxi.
A reflection of their people, their
   hospitality, their humbleness, their
   uncorrupted values, and their honesty.

Sitting in tranquility - by lake Yanxi.
Another experience of assertiveness and
   confirmation that negative propaganda
   assists the elites to divide and conquer.

Betty Smith Franklin
Maryland - USA

China

A street full of bicycles flows into Beijing's opacity.
Black hair, black eyes, thin bodies
All well-spaced
All intent on the pattern
Of shared, active space
Moving on and on,
Street to street, highway to highway.

On the sidewalk,
Old men balancing covered bird cages in each hand
Scurry-rock-scurry to proscribed benches on low walls
Where birds are discussed with the enthusiasm of owners
At Churchill Downs.

A squadron of old ladies (and one man) with cheap, over-size fans
Gleefully performs a drill team routine accompanied by drums.
When they are dismissed for a break,
A woman goes to the drums,
Beats the pattern.

People laugh, point.
The real drummers sit smoking, amused.

No wild birds singing, no sirens,
No subway rumbles in this part of Chaoyang District.
Only the splashes, swishes as wheels
Go through puddles, rivulets.
Engines drone--half the cars are quarantined each day
To show a better face of traffic
These weeks of hospitality.

Voices are loud--never are they modulated toward intimacy.
Any conversation is open to all.
Forty people advise simultaneously,
Deciphering instructions written for the taxi.

An unlikely candidate for English or for Chinese characters
(A woman in a ragged apron selling post cards at the Forbidden City)
Catches the mistake.

"Oh, the Workers' Stadium, not the Workers' Palace."
Forty laughs, forty faces contented
(They solved the riddle)
Flow away in jovial groups.

The driver repeats, "The Workers' Stadium, not the Workers' Palace."
Smiles, nods.
"Sorry."
We get back into the cab.

I take the seat of the foreigner,
A ghost,
Speeding into the milky light, alone.

Josephine Mascarenas Diaz
Illinois - USA

You Have a Voice

Speak Your Peace

Let It Be A Voice of Faith
Let It Be A Voice of Hope
And Most of All
Let It Be A Voice of Love
Because Love "Excels" Them All

I Do Not Wish To Offend Anyone
I Feel You Were All God Sent

And You All Have A Message
        To Bring Here
        To Bring Back Home
            To Your People
                To Your Women
                To Your Children
                To Your Men

You Have A Challenge Before You
And Each And Everyone of You
        Have The Vision,
            Have The Strength

Take Strategic, Efficient, And
        Effective Action

Let Us Be Leaders of Peace
Let Us Be As One
Let Us Be As Sisters
Let Us Be Connected
        As Peacemakers

Be Kind
Be Role Models

Be Teachers
Become Coaches
Become Mentors
Become A Good Friend
    First To Yourself
    And Then To All
    That You Can Touch
        With Unconditional
        Trust, Love, and Respect

And Never Lose Your Voice
Thru You And The Energies Of Others
You Will Create Synergy
        To Have Your Voice
        Heard Here,
            At Home,
        And Throughout The World!

God Bless.

Reflecting

Deborah S. Altman
Florida - USA

Beijing and Back

I've been to Beijing and back, so far and yet even farther.
Who says the world is shrinking? Whoever said that isn't thinking.
Or, at least is speaking propaganda.
How was your trip? you ask.
Did you have a wonderful time? A wonderful time?
How innocent we are here!
Yes, one can revel at the temples, the parks, the architecture ancient
When you can find them.
Surrounded by the cacophony of horns, people, bikes,
The ancient mystery sinks into the sidewalks,
To be resurrected only by trained tour guides.
Where's the pride? Where's the joy in displaying 5000 years of
     history?
Buried beneath the vendors stalls, the desire for the almighty yuan.
Buried under the hearts of the squalor dwellers
In tin-roofed huts held down by bricks and debris,
Yet, sprouting the angled spokes of antenna for TV.
Where's the gentle mystical mind, capable of calm in tumultuous
     environs?
It's muddled and huddled behind the smog
That clears only briefly after a rain.

I stopped my bike to photograph Mao's portrait,
Much larger than life near Tiananmen Square

When a soldier pressed me on.
When I pointed to others, Chinese, photographing,
He gestured only me to move on.
When I offered a toddler a photo of Florida parrots
His mother smiled, as he tossed it to the curb.
How natural for him, how absurd.
How the woman screeched when I parked my bike
Blocking what she perceived to be access to her stall
And wouldn't cease her dreadful squall until I moved out of earshot.
How the soldier avoided an answer to how to enter Tiananmen Square,
    surrounded by strategically constructed barricades,
As are all sidewalks and streets.
One may move only where instructed -- control is carefully directed.
Control hangs in the air like the smog,
You can see it, smell it, breathe it.
I do not criticize, only sympathize with the masses who must live it.
For the first time, I felt being treated differently based solely upon
    my appearance.
And I am so grateful for that difference,
To know I was merely a voyeur there
And that my difference, my passport, would return me here.

Huairou Women

Close encounters have changed my thoughts, ideas, regard for life.
Encounters with the Vietnamese women appealing for the end of our
    Cuban Blockade.
Encounters with the Peruvian women stopping for a photograph,
    only to parade off to an emergency meeting.
Encounters with the Laotian women lined up with bright smiles
    for the press.
With the Kuwaiti women demonstrating in full dress for release of
    their prisoners in Iraq.
With the Muslim women sharing a bench with Ronald McDonald.
Haitian women begging for acknowledgment of existence in the
    Dominican Republic.
Japanese women enlightening the world on female bondage
While Somali women open our eyes to female genital mutilation.

Women of 45 countries who arrived on the Peace Train,
    10,000 miles in 22 days.
The Indian, Tibetan, Nigerian, Salvadoran,
The Korean, Filipino, Pakistani, Australian.

One could not deny the theme,
"Look at the World Through Women's Eyes."
Eyes full of suffering, yet so hopeful here,
So loving, so open, so giving, but none serene.
So ready to share the strangeness of their ideas,
    customs, prayers for change.
The spirit of the event overcame all that seemed strange.
Smiles, hugs, and kisses may have been the only common language
But they served to communicate the anguish, the appeal for relief
    through change,
Through accomplishing the Forum motto:
    Equality, Development, Peace.

Chinese intervention did not affect the spirit.
Blocked crosswalks, unfinished buildings, mud, soldiers -
Only the media chose that focus for the sensationalism in it.

But the women, oh, the women, how gorgeous, every one.
They were the news, they were the muse of the world.
For a brief moment in history, they were given the stage
To express and create out of desperation and rage,
Which changed to the hope and promise of writing a new page.

The flame that came from Africa, Nairobi, ten years ago
Was passed ceremoniously in Beijing, as a symbol of things
    accomplished, but with many miles to go.
Who knows what was accomplished
What gains may come from this,
But if you believe in the power of the spirit
Thirty-five thousand voices in unison, hearts in agreement,
    minds in focus
Certainly have power to grab our earth machine and steer it.

Mehri Shah Hosseini
IRAN

Huairou: City of Kindness

Huairou the city of kindness, the faith --
In your arms was the place of five continents' women.

Your sky let the drops of generosity
on our head.

Your beautiful sun gave the warmness
to our heart.

You were the class of love, friendship,
lessons to reborn.

You gave us the gift of peace, hope
and equality to develop.

And we, the daughters of Eve,
give you our kind smiles.

Huairou, I've Missed You

for your kind people, crowded streets, the
ones who were selling the handcrafts of
those hard women or men workers.

For those children waving their little
charming hands with their shiny eyes of
hospitality.

Huairou, I've missed you for your streets
of green trees rising in the sky, together
with us praying for peace, equality, development.

For your different workshops, teaching unity.

For your crowded nights filled by music.

Huairou, you got to be the sign of manners,
people's character of five continents.

And I framed this in my mind,
hung it to the wall of my heart.

Veronica L. Williams Sanders
Texas - USA

Have You Been to the Wall?

Have you been to the Wall
all those voices did shout
The Wall? Well, which wall
Are you talking about?

Why the Great Wall of China
What other wall do you know?
And if there's another
Where else did you go?

Yes, I toured the Great Wall
With its height and its depth
But was most overwhelmed
And with awesomeness swept

By the Great Wall of Women
With its ebb and its flow -
It encircles the world
The Great Wall N.G.O.

It's the wall that encompasses
Our feelings, emotions
It's the only wall I know of
That marches thru oceans

It's the wall that cries tears
Tells of joys, tells of sorrows
It's the wall that encourages
And gives hope for tomorrow

It's a wall that brings laughter
And gifts from afar
Shouting out: You're important
Whomever you are.

It's a wall that keeps building -
Breaking barriers with a touch
As it rings out the message
You are loved very much.

It's a wall that the media
Wouldn't dare to explore;
As they scale negativity
It cries "peace" all the more.

Its colors are varied
With a multiple hue
And you know in an instant
It does include you.

Yes, I toured the Great Wall
Found it awesome to see
Yet it's not that impression
That lingers with me.

Understand me when I say
That it was a great start
But the N.G.O. Wall
Left its mark on my heart.

I am not the same woman
I was weeks before
I walked up to this wall
That has taught me to soar

I've been taught I am special
That I'm loved, that I give
I'll remember this message
As long as I live.

I will teach it to others
So their spirits won't fall
And together we'll cross oceans
As the N.G.O. Wall.

Indira Y. Junghare
Minnesota - USA

The Great Wall *(in Marathi)*

चिनी भिंत

वाटे ती भिंत बालीका ऊषेच्या कडेवर
झुर ती सिंहीणी मध्यान्हाच्या मांडीवर
शहाणी ती भार्या संध्येच्या छायेत
पकित ती वृध्दा निशेच्या नशेत

न्हाते ती पर्जन्याच्या रिमझिमपीत
निद्रीते ती हिमाच्या शुभ्र शालीत
घाली ती सुवर्ण पर्णांची चोळी शरदांत
हेंट रान फुलांची वसंतात

नागिणीवत् लचके तिचे अवयाणु
नागिणीवत् चमके तिची तेलकट तनू
कुठ रोड, कुठ जाड
कुठ टोंवरांच्या गाठी अवघड

मोठी भिंत भासे चिनी जनांस डोंगन
माझ्या मनी मात्र ती महा नागिण
पर्वती घाली वळसा ऊंच उडी मारुन
धरी प्रियकर घट्ट आवळुन

जणु ते प्रेमाचे अलिंगण
जणु ते प्रेमरसाचें संकेतन
जाती धर्मला धरुन
आकाशाच्या निळ्या दुलईखालून

सुंदर दिसे ती भिंत निसर्ग सान्निध्यांत
सुंदर दिसे ती भिंत पर्वताच्या बाहुत
शुभ्र तिचा स्कर्ट हरित त्याचा शर्ट
जोडी दोघांची खरीच उत्कृष्ट

रक्षिली तिन बहु चीनी राज्यें
शत्रुच्या क्रुर आक्रमांतुन
दिन रात्र रक्षक बनुन
मोठ्या भक्तिनं, मोठ्या कष्टानं

Indira Y. Junghare
Minnesota - USA

The Great Wall
  for Anjira

A child the Wall looks in the dawn's lap
A lioness in the noon's wrath
A wise lady is she in the dusk's darkness
a tired woman in the night's conquest

In rain's pearly shower she bathes
In snow's white shawl she rests
A golden-leafy blouse she wears in autumn
A hat of pretty buds in spring's blossom

Like a queen cobra she flows
Like an oily snake she glows
Silky shiny skin, smooth wavy fins
Stony towers shape her bony wings

The Great Wall is a big dragon to the Chinese
But a huge she-cobra to me
Soaring high the majestic mountain she winds
Embracing tight the mystical lover she binds

It is a lover's embrace
The feature of love's make
Among the kingdom of snakes
Under the sky's blue lace

Charming she looks in nature's chamber
Enticing she seems on mountain's shoulder
Snow-white is her skirt, bluish-green is her lover's shirt
The pair is uniquely the first

Many China's kingdoms she protected
When the enemies harshly invaded
By becoming a faithful guardian
Serving with loyalty and devotion

बनुन प्रवाशांची शिक्षकीण
देई त्यांना चीनी संस्कृतीचे ज्ञान
सही लाखो लोकांची याद्त्राण
सही त्रास बहु वर्षांपासुन

बनुन माझी मैत्रीण
दिलीस मज अनंताची जाण
दिलेस मज निसर्गांचे ज्ञान
दिलेस मज प्रियकराचे दर्शन

लग बग बघितली चिनी भिंत
चढ चढली पाय-या ऊंच
फुट फुटले शरीरी रोमांच
जणू जीवलगासाठी जीव होई विरक्त

नकळत पडले मी तिच्या प्रियकराच्या प्रेमांत
सहज रमले मी त्याच्या मधुर मोहांत
क्षणभर हरले भान निसर्गाच्या मिठींत
दुबदुब-दुबले मी ब्रम्हाच्या आनंदात

भिंतीस नसावी क्षणिक भिती
तिच्या प्रियकराच्या बहु प्रेयसी
लाखो येती अन् लाखो जाती
किंतु तीच त्याची एकमेव सखी

भव्य भींत मानवाचा पराक्रम
भव्य पर्वत निसर्गांचे लेण
असे का ती निसर्ग मानव स्पर्धा कसुन?
ना, ते प्रकृती पुरूषाचे प्रेमबंधन
आत्मा-परमात्मा ह्यांचे मीलन

भींत-प्रवास तो तीर्थ मात्रेचा
प्रयत्न तो आत्मशांतीचा
अनुभव तो सत्-चित् आनंदाचा
योगायोग तो भाग्याचा

A guru to the ascenders
She teaches them the Chinese culture
Patiently she endures their footwear
Devotionally she serves for years

As a friend, she awakened my soul's inspiration
Making me aware of the Infinite's abstraction
Making me conscious of the Nature's absolutism
Filling my mind with the Ultimate's admiration

I climbed the Wall with ease
Ascending the steps with energy release
Exploded my limbs with romantic inspiration
As if I was longing for my beloved's vision

Unaware I fell in love with her majestic lover
Momentarily I was caught by mountain's stare
Suddenly I lost my sanity in nature's divine grace
Becoming one with Cosmic Consciousness

None or nothing the Wall fears
Her lover has millions of affairs
Millions of mistresses ascend and descend
She alone ultimately transcends

The Great Wall is human creation
The lofty mountain is nature's donation
Are the Man and the Nature in competition?
Nay, they present Mind and Matter's connection
Man and Nature's sacred relation

The journey to the Wall was a pilgrimage
The spirit's revival is a human privilege
Union with Pure Consciousness and Bliss
Must have been a part of my karmic merit

Jyoti Mhapsekar
INDIA

We Women Hold Half the Sky *(in Marathi)*

अर्धे आकाश पेलणाऱ्या आम्ही स्त्रिया, आम्ही स्त्रिया

इतिहासाच्या पानांनी अदृश्य आम्हां ठेविले
जरी आम्ही निर्मिक विश्वाच्या, श्रम आमुचे न कोणा दिसले
गत शतकाच्या जागरणाने जाग आम्हाला आली
निर्भय होऊनी नवशतकाला जाऊ आता सामोऱ्या
आम्ही स्त्रिया, आम्ही स्त्रिया . .

शिक्षणाने स्त्री जीवनाला दिला वेगळा अर्थ
ज्ञानज्योत लावून करू आम्ही प्रत्येकीस समर्थ
निर्णयक्षम होऊ करू आम्ही भगिनीभावा सार्थ
स्वाभिमान अन् सन्मानाने जगण्या धडपडणाऱ्या
आम्ही स्त्रिया, आम्ही स्त्रिया . .

हक्कासाठी जागरूक आम्ही न चुकू कर्तव्याला
शतक उद्याचे आमुचे याची जाणीव असे आम्हाला.
समर्थ आमुचे हात उद्याचे भविष्य घडविण्याला . .
पुरुषांची घेऊनी साथ हे जग सुंदर करणाऱ्या
आम्ही स्त्रिया, आम्ही स्त्रिया . .

समानता हे ध्येय आमुचे, पण केवळ तितुके नाही
भूक गरीबी वर्णभेद हिंसेशीही आमुची लढाई
निसर्ग मानव समतोलाची आसही आमुच्या हृदयी.
विकास - समता विश्वशांती या ध्येया नित जपणाऱ्या
आम्ही स्त्रिया, आम्ही स्त्रिया . .

66 - Seeing the World

Jyoti Mhapsekar
INDIA

We Women Hold Half the Sky
(English translation by Sharada Sathe)

We women hold half the sky
    On our shoulders
With heads held high
And march towards a better future.

    Invisible in history as humans
We are not mere wives or mothers
    Or daughters or sisters
Nor are we weaklings of nature
Forgotten are with ease
    Our endless labours
    Of thousands of years
    The bells of reawakening of last century
    Ringing high in our ears
    We are no more in slumber
    Let us join hands
    With confidence newly acquired
    And march towards a better future.

    The light of learning and wisdom
    Kindles our hearts with hopes afresh
    We are literate and fearless
    Empowered to decide for ourselves
    With dignity and self respect
    We decorate the life elixir
    And march towards a better future.

Let us seize our rights
And not forget our duties
    The future belongs to us
The powerful shoulders
With men by our side
We desire to make this planet
    Beautiful and fair

Jyoti Mhapsekar
INDIA

We Women Hold Half the Sky *(in Hindi)*

लें कंधोंपर आधा आकाश

लें कंधोंपर आधा आकाश सरको उठाके चलें
हम विश्वकी महिला इक्कीसवी सदी की ओर चलें

अतीत के पन्नोंमें हम सब है गुमसुम
केवल माता या ना अबला । हमी भी हैं मानव सक्षम
आसानीसे भूल गये वो । हमने उठाये सदियोंसे श्रम
जन जागरसे पिछली सदी की । जाग उठी हम जाग उठी
आओ मिलकर नये विश्वाससे लें हाथों मे हाथ चलें

शिक्षा ज्ञान का दिया जला । जीवनको नव अर्थ मिला
साक्षर होगी नीडर होगी । निर्णय काबिल नारी होगी
स्वाभिमानसे और सम्मान से जीवन सजाने चलें

हक तो हमारा लेके रहेंगे
कर्तव्य भी नही भूलेंगे
आनेवाली सदी हमारी ।हमें खबर है बाहु सबल है
मर्दों के साथ इस धरती को सुंदर बनाने चलें

समानता है ध्येय हमारा । पर बस नही उतनाही
भूख, गरीबी, वर्ण भेद । और हिंसासे है ये लड़ाई
निसर्ग मानव संतुलन हो । तबही होगा सफल ये जीवन
विकास, समता, विश्वशांती का नारा लगांते चलें

And march towards a better future.

For equality do we strive
And fight to end poverty and hunger
And violence and racial strife

We strive for life meaningful
Thru balance of man and nature
Here is our clarion call
For Development, Equality and World Peace
    To march towards a better future.

This poem, written for the N.G.O. Forum, has become the theme song of S.N.D.T., the only women's university in India. It was first written in Marathi, a language of the state of Maharashtra, and later translated into Hindi, the national language. The song was included in the cultural program presented by India on the Kumba stage in Huairou at the N.G.O. Forum. It was published in the March 1995 issue of the magazine PRERAK LALKARI (CLARION CALL).

The Editors

Judy Forbister
CANADA

Think Wisely

There is a reason
though not totally clear,
for my obsession to be part
of the Beijing affair:

To unite with my sisters
so very diverse,
and work for the girl child
of our small universe.

The earth is so small
and I now realize,
that gains sought in Canada
may materialize,

not only in changes
for my homeland and me,
but have far reaching consequences
for my sisters 'cross the sea.

Thus I wish to think wisely
before actions I take,
Will the impact of my movement
a better world make?

Think wisely, dear sisters,
when you take up the fight,
Will the changes you fight for
improve ALL OUR plight?

I ask you, dear sisters
think what needs to be done,
DO NOT ACCEPT the web
that patriarchy has spun.

Spin a new web
strong, interlocking with peace,
so that inequality and oppression
of the girl child will cease.

Julanne Sweeney
AUSTRALIA

Not Exactly.....

This is not exactly where I want to be
At 2 pm on the first day of October
Chasing squarking geese from the stage at Warrina Lakes
Waiting for would-be poets and a performer.

I could be at Mena Creek planting quondongs
Dying to break out of foam plastic into earthy beds.
I could be floating down the River Li near beautiful Guilin
Considering cormorants, capitalism; sipping jasmine tea....

This is not exactly where I want to be
calculating takings under a Leichhardt tree like a poetonomic
       rationalist
Stripping the joy from Innisfail and Cracow memories
In the workshop's balmy scene.

But................ if this is not exactly where I want to be
I COULD be struggling for survival in Ruanda
Trying to replant seeds among the landmines with one arm.

I could be a child of 800 in Bosnia who can't find either my mum or
       dad
I could be Maeve McGoldrick who's challenging the Irish government
       for not protecting her
Night after thumping night.

So if this is not exactly where I want to be
I'm pretty stupid to be telling it out loud to you
In this land of peace and plenty.

Patricia Bray
Minnesota - USA

Communion: Beijing '95

Dedicated to all those who read from right to left, left to right
and to those who can only listen.

30,000

women's souls

touched

A spiritual orgasm

shook

THE EARTH

The Passion

creating

feeling

United!

Committed

to action

Joining

hands

Linking

souls

Moving

forward

Hearts

suffering

The violence

of the status

Quo   Go!

Never

Turning back

Alive

        Women

               Weaving

                       The World

T--O--G--E--T--H--E--R---

Marilyn M. Cuneo
Minnesota - USA

Born in Huairou
> *September 1995*

It's alive now.
Can you hear it?
> A bolder voice
> A sharper tone
> A stronger word

Can you hear it?

It's alive now.
Can you see it?
> A face aglow
> A quickened step
> A head held high

Can you see it?

It's alive now.
Can you feel it?
> A hope-filled heart
> A mind alert
> A strengthened will.

Can you feel it?

It's alive now.
WOMAN SPIRIT!
Loosed upon Earth
from the chaos
that was China.
Weaving its way
through young and old.
Binding us in a
mission of love:

> Take back the world
> and make it ours
> to heal the wounds.

> Take back the world
> and make it ours
> to grow in peace

> Take back the world
> and make it ours
> to live in health.

> Take back the world
> and make it ours
> to show the way.

> Take back the world
> and make it ours
> to humanize.

WOMAN SPIRIT.
It's alive now.
Does it move you?

Unite with it!
Live it! Spread it!

It's alive now.

Holly Sloan
New York - USA

To Be Heard

Refugees

At my first session in Huairou I met a young woman.
She caught my attention when she thanked god that she was a refugee.
Outside her homeland's borders she patiently organizes people--hoping
that one day the current government will fall and her sisters and brothers will live free...

In one soft, swift moment, an older woman rose, her eyes turned away
from me. Her veil and dress surround her secrets--helping to keep the
story she is eager to tell inside. HER SISTERS MUST BE PROTECT-
ED, SHE MUST NOT SAY TOO MUCH--in a whisper, she begs the
young woman speaking to stop asking about the displaced women and
men in her nation. Voice shaking, she prays that we will leave those
inside to the struggle-- "I know that people are dying, we are working
within, your efforts and concerns bring only harm to the ones we are
trying to free--please trust us--trust that we know--trust that we are acting."

> *I am walking home from work in New York City,*
> *as I do on most evenings.*
> *I pass the couple who live under the awning of First Avenue,*
> *two blocks from the United Nations. Run off in the morning,*
> *they are back to the familiar cement, organizing their blankets*
> *and belongings, discussing their day and preparing a meal--*
> *as I pass, respectfully trying not to disturb, I hope that it will*
> *be cloudy tonight--clouds will keep some of the fall chill away*
> *as they sleep.*
>
> *Trust that we know, trust that we are acting ... Quietly I slip*
> *away.*

Mothers

Everyday they marched in black, twenty maybe fifty.
Free in Beijing to walk together, to conspire and cry.
They represent millions, millions of women who have lost their loves,

their sons and daughters--in prisons, in wars, in shallow graves or graves of hundreds. Everyday they marched--back home they will march in their minds, cry into the dirt--trusting we heard, trusting someone knows, trusting someone is acting.

Lawyers Committee on Human Rights

"We must teach our children to live in struggle"--her voice echoed to the back of the hot crowded classroom-- "We must celebrate struggle." The audience stood, arms in the air, heads thrown back as they revealed and renewed their trust in their collective struggle for human rights--"It will not come for us, nor perhaps for our children, but we must resist the comfort that our progress provides and live in the discomfort of truth..."

Indigenous Peoples Network

"We are lawyers, we are professors, and accountants and business women. We have embraced the titles and veils the European culture values--we have done this so we will be heard. You cannot use our lack of education, your unfamiliarity with our lifestyles or our savagery to distance us--we are among you now. Will you join us in speaking the truth, acknowledging the real history of indigenous people? We trust you to hear--to step towards us and our reality--please speak the truth with us... We have made room for you in our lives, please make room for us in yours."

I had seen them in the Indigenous Peoples Network caucus--women with fierce commitment, gentle in their inclusiveness, secure in the integrity of their agenda --these were women to be taken seriously. Two sisters, Maya by heritage and steeped in the arts and prejudice of Brooklyn discrimination, it was no surprise that they used song and theater to be heard. They emerged from the front of the room and took control. They sang and acted out childhood fantasies, arguing who would play the prince this time, and showed the audience the wholeness of their experiences, the range of their emotions and of our oneness as women, Yes, these were women to be taken seriously. Together we laughed for hours.

Two Women

They stood not more than a foot apart.
"Excuse me, you say that I am disturbing you--well that is exactly what

I come to Beijing to do." She does not retreat, she will be heard, she may not be able to save all women from abuse and inequality, but she surely can convince this lone woman of the evils her religion has perpetrated against her--perhaps, it is to save this one woman that she journeyed to Beijing...

The veiled woman averts her eyes, she wants to run, but the other is locked to her every movement--"Perhaps I should not have come, this is what my mother was afraid of"-- words are lost--choked in fear and emotion--"I promised myself that I would not run from those who attack my way of life--seek to discredit my god--I must make her hear."

In a synchronized moment I see them scream to the sky. I felt I was intruding, I could not hear the words, but their bodies were heaving with passion--I was afraid--I moved away.

> *First Avenue is closed, lined with limousines and chauffeurs waiting to take the dignitaries back to their hotels after the 50th anniversary celebration of the United Nations.*

> *The streets are clean and the homeless couple who make their shelter on 43rd Street will be looking for another place to sleep tonight. As I pass by, I wonder what kind of difference this celebration will make in the lives of the refugees, the homeless, the disenfranchised. I wonder if the spirit of the women I met in Huairou is with the delegates. I wonder if they are heard.*

> *Trust that we know, trust that we are acting.*

(Submitted by the Association of Junior Leagues International, Inc.)

Susu Jeffrey
Minnesota - USA

Beijing Around the Earth

It was not exotic
the Beijing conference;
40,000 women spoke, listened
& demonstrated in front of the
mainstream world press.

Hey, I went to Beijing
for the Women's Conference
to see the sisters
to hear the news
to take notes
& come back
& tell you.
    I went around the world.
    I went around & around
    this beautiful
          Earth.
You can't own Her.
Because if you think
you could own Land
you might think
you could own
    anything.
People--
are not for sale.
Land is not for sale
land is not a dump.
Land is for living on.
Tomorrow
is not for sale.
It's now
& it belongs to everybody.
It's the new ethic.

Intellectual property
is air.

It's ideas.
Share the air.
Don't be a pimp.
It's the new ethic.

Sisters, I looked
& you   know
I ap*preciate*
the sisters.
I saw sisters
from all over the world--
believe me I went
looking, around
& I couldn't see
by looking
who had been raped.

I met Ayse
who was tortured
in Istanbul, Turkey
they torture women
    It is like an operation.
In parts of Africa
a wife cannot refuse
marital "rights"
to her husband
    with AIDS.
Burning
is torture used
all over the world
torture

is a violation of Human Rights.
Women's rights are
Human Rights.
It was voted on
& it **is** policy
around the world.

You can point

to a paper
with the words
Women's rights are Human Rights.
Rape is a war crime.
There is war
wherever a woman is raped
it is war
against women.
We declare
war is over!
You cannot rape
you cannot own
            people, land, air--
we have equality
in mind.
A new millennium.
A new astro age
a new ethic--
Human Rights
means each person
on this beautiful blue
            Earth
is just like
     you.
We're alike
so much
like music
everybody
from all over
the Earth sings.

If you go
da-da-da, da-da, da
you just said *yes*
in Russian
six times.
I heard it
on the train
from Finland
on the Baltic Sea

the waves on the rocks
to Hong Kong
on the South China Sea
the waves
of people
of ideas about
  what's wrong
& what we can do about it.
Stop!
You cannot own
minds or hearts, women or children,
you can be a partner.
Tomorrow
is not quite here.
So let's save   time
          the economy
               lives
            the soil
practice now
Human Rights,
it's survival.

233 women from 42 countries
on the Peace Train.
There is birch forest
from Helsinki, Finland
to St. Petersburg, Russia.
Trees don't observe
the border
the difference between--
  is not the land.
The minute you cross
from Finland to Russia
you can see it
    how a military budget
bleeds prosperity.
A rougher ride
on the train tracks
a few bruises
the clatter

another decibel.
Classrooms in America
getting rougher & louder
too. Pentagon
is the only department
got more
than it asked for.
St. Petersburg
on the fast Neva River,
from here till home
all of us, all the time
drink bottled water
but eat the fish
& see rivers of soot in the skies.
It is unnatural for animals
to shit in the drinking water.
We are prisoners of habit.

Pollution in St. Petersburg
dulls its pastel beauty.
The mayor's feminist representative
has been doing the job
16 years.
Bureaucracy survives politics
but the KGB straitjacket
on Russian faces
is removed.
They speak with heart
& with a little vodka
we communicate--
& I remember growing up afraid.

Kiev on the Dnepr River
is the most beautiful
city I will see
this summer.
Scenery interrupts everything
on the train:
meals, workshops
sleeping, talking.

Postcards roll by.
I have stopped
blinking.

We are met with flowers,
traditional singing, bread & salt,
a band.
Kiev, Ukraine, is dying.
They have plenty to eat
but the nuke at Chernobyl
60 miles upstream
is still melting down.
Kiev has lost
a third of its population
every pregnancy is a heartbreak
decision.
Just like Las Vegas--
equivalent to a chest X-ray
everyday
    declare Peace
with Earth.
We have women of child-bearing
age with us.
We are treated as diplomat-heroines.
Nobody comes to Kiev
anymore.

They wake us up
in Romania
4:30 am
in the poorest country in Europe
the *passport control* guy gets the giggles.
Ceausescu is gone
& my African-American roommate
gives him my passport
& he cannot believe his eyes
    in the mountains
    with the trees
    past a no-man's-land
    between people who live

    in the same landscape
Is this you? he asks
looks at the picture
  looks at her
   looks at the picture
    looks at her
Of course it's me you fool.
It's 4:30 in the morning
you woke us up
again--
Yes. Yes, it's me.
Stamp it. Just
stamp it.

Where are we?
--Oh.
Susu get up.
Wake up.
Sit up.
Let this man
see your face
girl. Get up
now
I learned a lot
about racism.
America is more guilty of racism
than O.J. is of murder.

Peace.
Whatever you need
   dignity-food-shelter-
   health care-education-
   a job-justice
you get more
sooner
with peace.
Demand
Peace.
In Yugoslavia
people have lived together

along the Danube watershed
since prehistory.
Romania & Bulgaria
are going broke
from the embargo
on the Yugoslav civil war--
only weapons get through.

In Sofia, Bulgaria & Istanbul, Turkey
Sveta Sofia & Hagia Sofia
are both ochre, blood
life-colored churches
built on Sacred Land
on ancient trade routes.
I think they were oracle
sites. I leave crystals.

I begin eating aspirins
for breakfast
a day after the Chinese underground
nuclear test at Lop Nor.
The radiation reached Almaty
Kazakhstan in four hours.
We arrive the day before
the nuclear rainfall.
I leave my umbrella.
Every smoke stack across
eastern Europe
central Asia & China
needs a scrubber
& every car, bus & truck
pours scum.
I got some new ideas
about foreign aid.
The Kazakhs got nuked
by the government
    across the border--
we call them
illegal aliens
& they can't get

the same benefits I get
on this same
piece of topography.
The new ethic
is inalienable rights.
Human Rights.

Welcome to the People's
Republic of China--
house arrest
on the Peace Train
23-hours & 40-minutes a day
with two exercise breaks
on a railroad platform closed
to the people
who wear masks
   the men neutral
   women with a
   have-a-nice-day- smile.
Political freedom
is a Human Right.

Not once in China
did I fear rape.
I never
   looked under the car
before getting in.
Sino security tripped
all my hotel luggage traps
but I got the Tibetan
torture documentation
past customs
& presented at Huairou.

Fascism is so obvious
in a foreign land
so I meditated
on fascism at home:
   sexual abuse
   the single media message

tape loop
on every station
invisible camera surveillance
in every store
on every freeway
telephones & telecommunications
& the United DeFence Industries
threatened by hacker warriors,
unemployment
a breast cancer epidemic
homelessness
& the executive god, Go-Go
who shows up
as leather heart tissue
in US autopsies.
Privacy means you can't see them.
Freedom means don't get noticed.
You can't have democracy
& nuclear waste
at the same time
at the same place.
My sister says
I'm too negative.
The messenger
notices cracks in the pavement.
The Earth isn't going to die,
it's people.

I missed my yard.
When Casa Blanca lilies
bloom, they turn
me into an animal
    I can see
    with my nose
& I missed my friends.
All of eastern Europe
central Asia
northern China
August & part of September
went by on the train

my body
focused into an eye eating scenery:
Baltic, forest, wetlands
fields of wheat, corn, rice
patches of gardens
streams, lakes, rivers
villages, cities, people
     selling things
mountain waters
irrigating the Ergene Valley
     in Turkey.
I swam the Baltic Sea
& the Black Sea
     despite the cholera scare,
washed my hair in Mother Volga
& the prairie climbed to high plains
& dry mountains with glacier peaks
& the desert, the great
red Gobi Desert
went on for days.
China's about the size
of the US
with five times the population.
TIANANMEN, I said--
a papier-mache Goddess of Liberty
thousands of people slaughtered
by the People's Army--
WHAT? said the guide.
*Oh you mean
the Tiananmen Square Event.
It was only 23 people.* *
90-percent of China is not
farm-able-- it's actually those misty mountains
on silk scroll paintings
I thought were imaginary landscapes
or, it's desert.
A billion people live in the green belt
along the waxing moon-shaped
Pacific rim.
Seven weeks across eastern Europe

& China, I never saw
a fat person.
Food issues
only bless
a cornucopia society.
Off Japan our flight home
circumnavigated a typhoon
& circled Anchorage, Alaska at 18,000-feet
while the sun rose
below on Mt. McKinley
    from gray through pink to yellow.
Hey, I went to Beijing
for the Women's Conference
through 9 nations & 24
time zones, jamming
around the world
& I saw fascism abroad
& racism at home
the press as a tranquilizer
everywhere
  the sun rises, sets & beauty
everyone sings
around this living
              Earth
we need not extinct ourselves;
it's the new ethic.

*23 *students* were massacred during the Tiananmen Square Event.
Estimates for total deaths vary:

Russian report	10,000 killed
TIME Magazine	5,000
Amnesty International	700-3,000
NY TIMES	400-800

PART II
RAISING OUR VOICES BOLDLY

INTRODUCTION

Many of the poems we received came from people who did not go to the Beijing Conference, but who wanted to unite their voices with the rising chorus of global concern over the stifling ways women experience the world in their lives.

We hear women challenging, encouraging, strengthening, empowering each other as they relate their stories and express their feelings. In these poems women reach out to each other, claiming kinship as sisters from all four corners of the earth. Underlying their differences they see a commonality of interests and experiences which connects them and gives them a base of hope on which to construct a more peaceful, productive, nourishing, sustainable future, not just for themselves, but for all of humanity. This is the goal proclaimed in the Beijing Declaration as a preface to the Platform for Action, the final document agreed upon by 189 nations at the UN 4th World Conference on Women, September 15, 1995.

Woman to Woman

Nicole Cheetham
Washington, D.C. - USA

Lucky to Be a Woman

Blessed are we who are women
Why would we want to be anything else?

We are the strong ones
We are the peaceful ones
We are the resourceful ones
We are the giving ones

Even with injustice
Even with pain

We survive
And this is why we are different

We have the gift of inner-strength
which allows us to persevere
And we share this collectively
as we empower ourselves

So sisters, let us congratulate ourselves for being women
Let us be proud
And let us be happy
for who we are
Why would we want to be anything else?

Susal Stebbins
Minnesota - USA

Fire

This woman is Fire.
This woman is Eternal Flame.
She cannot be extinguished;
She cannot be contained.
Love ignites her.
Love is her fuel.
She burns through injustice
and warms the world.

Stacy M. Lass
Minnesota - USA

Woman

Woman,
with eyes of fire
and words of silence
Stare outside your window
past the cold wet day
past these unforgiving stormclouds
look again to the stars
of which you were born
their brilliance twinkles
and dances in your eyes.
Beautiful woman,
as a tear falls to your warm breast
sing songs to the sky about
pictures in the heightless clouds
Woman,
who is much too beautiful for
this brutal world,
one day you shall fly.
Woman, wrapped in linen cloth

flowing in the gentle breeze
in the glow of the moonlight.
Woman,
sleep on the shores,
upon these burning banks
become united with your soaring spirit.

Jody Johnson
Minnesota - USA

The Strength of Women

Women grieve strongly
shoulders heaving with wrenching sobs
pain an open raw heat
released in waves of emotional energy.
This is not weakness.
Women stand and survive
the overwhelming force of their own agony,
allowing the intensity of their loss
to change them, and in the process
redefining the negative into the difficult,
but positive.
Women absorb and evolve
rather than standing rigidly and breaking.
They recreate themselves,
straining with the labor of their lives
to birth new meaning.

Emily Gottschalk
Minnesota - USA

Yellow Butterflies

Yellow butterflies dance around my soul,
   my heart.
Growing, learning,
   striving to understand what it is to be a woman.
Cannot look to my elders.
   The elders around me have forgotten.
Cannot look to my children.
   They look to me.
Must look to the yellow butterflies that
   flutter and laugh within me.

Susan Jensen
Minnesota - USA

Being I am

I am a Shakti
Dancing being
Arms linking the group heart-soul.

I am a Gorgon
Multi-limbed.
Spinning in the vortexes of time.

I am an Earth Woman.
I am an Earth Mother.
My orifices have been forced and rent,
My limbs pinned and bound,
Straight-jacketed,
Like the meandering arms of so many rivers,
In forced beds of formed concrete,
And the tall ones limbs-
Roots and branches,

Severed, plundered,
Energy forcing steel teeth and iron chains,
And the others, on legs and wings...

And I am a Thought Woman,
All that ever was, and is, and will be.

In all this that I am,
I will focus through me all energies,
So loosely and heavily expended
In force and bondage,
In control and dominance

And I will dissolve them
Into the life-sustaining universe.
I will stretch and flex into the mysteries,
Energizing the elements.

For I am free,
And all intent can be transformed.

Mary Cee
Minnesota - USA

River/Woman Meditation

The river is ever the same,
            ever different,
            ever changing.

So is woman:
        She sparkles in the sunlight of appreciation.
        She dances with the winds of change.
        She nourishes life
            both within her being
            and in her surroundings
                encouraging growth.
        She moves with steady sure power

eroding the hardness of men.
When she is dammed,
　　　she rises and gains power
When she is mildly polluted,
　　　she purifies herself.
She flows into the sea of all-that-is, and
Finally,
　　　　she merges with the Infinite.

Anonymous

We Are Women

We build the foundation
to the society that shuns us
We are the bringers of life
creators of beauty
forgotten, slaughtered, punished.
We, in our misery,
cut each other down.
Capable of so much, willing
to do much more!
We are women.
We will be oppressed no more.

Helen Gaebe
Minnesota - USA

Democracy Rising

My sister I call to you
Across the water.
Hear my voice
Rising from
The place of Birthing
Rising from the Sea.

My daughter is with you.
As I have birthed her
So she has birthed me.

My sister I call to you
Across the water.
Hear my voice
Rising from
The place of Birthing
Rising from the Earth.

My daughter is with you.
As I have fed her
So she has fed me.

My sister I call to you
Across the water.
Hear my voice
Rising from
The place of Birthing
Rising from the Air.

My daughter is with you.
As I have wept for her,
So she has wept for me.

My sister I call to you
Across the water.

Hear my voice
Rising from
The place of Birthing
Rising from the Fire.

My daughter is with you.
As I am with her
So she is with me.
As I am with you
So you are with me.

My sister I call to you
Across the water.
My sister I call to you
Across the heavens.

Take my heart.
Give it to our daughter
As I have died in her
So she has died in me.

My daughter was in the Peace Corps in Togo, West Africa. Togo was undergoing civil strife and there had been no contact with the outside world for several months. My daughter called on the morning of December 24 at 5:00 a.m. to tell me she was safe and what she had experienced.

Rosa Bogar
Minnesota - USA

Sisters

Hands	reaching	must touch
Hearts	beating	must feel
Eyes	looking	must see

we are sisters
of
the universe
we MUST converse

Shirley Franklin-Gummadi
Minnesota - USA

Sisters

Sister
You opened your heart one day
poured out your love
and your longing to be heard.
I listened
and knew our bond.
Too soon
the dinner had to be stirred
you shut your heart
and denied you'd said a thing.
Still, listening,
I know our bond.

Joan M. Drury
Minnesota - USA

Another Fat Poem

women
are obsessed with fat:
>they're afraid of fat
>afraid of plump-donut-midriffs
>afraid of long-john-thighs
>afraid of bismarck-buttocks

they remember Ruben's women:
>women with soft full bodies
>swollen sensuality
>enticing flesh
>spilling over the edges of canvas

and moan about being born
in the wrong century

women forget the pluses of fat:
>forget that fat keeps them warm in the winter
>forget that fat means no spiky bones
>forget that fat means no fresh men with stale lines

instead:
>women long for stringbean bodies
>rhubarb-rib-cages
>celery-thighs
>spinach-leaf-bottoms
>sliced-beet-bosoms

women are so denied flesh
they're afraid of any excess

Jessie Craig
Minnesota - USA

The Voice Speaks

The voice speaks silence of women waiting
    in dark alleyways
The healer speaks. Where is she coming from?
The woman waits - whole - a circle
    surrounding her body.
A woman waits.
What is she afraid of?
The circle keeps her whole.
Dark alleyways possess many secrets.
The secrets of shame and oppression.
Who are we?
The woman waits.
The circle becomes - a light - her own
    illumination.
And she rests in it.
Lets it consume her.
The light becomes her body.
And she learns to listen to it.

Liz Dodson
Minnesota - USA

Dance of Connection

Melanie was my aunt....
She became La Melanita my muse,
my morning star, my light
When she put on her dancing shoes.....
she became part of the deep, renewing
holy river.....
the light that shines into darkness
the spirit that flows from one woman to

the next and dances
on and on
If it feels right
you are the music
you dance the dance of life.

Ann E Gerike
Minnesota - USA

To Younger Women
A Prayer for Us All

We are your mothers and grandmothers,
Your great-grandmothers, your great-great grandmothers,
Your aunts and great-aunts and great-great aunts,
Your older sisters, your spirit sisters.

You have come from our bodies.
You have come from the bodies of our daughters,
Or our daughters-in-law.
You have come from the bodies of our granddaughters,
Or the bodies of our sisters, our nieces, our great-nieces,
Our friends' daughters, their daughters, their friends.

With you, we form a chain.
Each link in the chain is vital.
Each is of equal value.
Each has its own strengths.

Each link in the chain is beautiful.

May our connections not be broken.
May we learn from one another.
May we help and encourage and support one another.
May we make the world a better place for one another.

May our connections not be broken.
May we be at peace.

Girl Child

Anonymous

Untitled

十六芳龄已孤身，
只因家贫又属女，
轻浅婚略中学托，
飘落他乡谋新生。

谎言与我同出生，
灾难跟我步步紧，
母亲害怕而撒谎，
岂知父亲是男儿。

谎言被揭父亲狂，
女儿使他大失望，
一怒之下而出走，
造下母女孤苦伶。

一身包袱一身罪，
拆散家庭伤母心；
怨谁赐我女儿身，
脆说还我女儿权！

Anonymous

*In the summer of 1993, I went back to China after six and a half years'
absence. While staying in a small lodging house in a town in
Southeast China, I met a girl from Sichuan, Deng Xiao-ping's home-
town. She was employed at the family-run lodging house as a cham-
bermaid to clean guest rooms. Here is her story:*

Untitled

Prime sixteen, alone in the world,
I am poor and woman.
Negligence of bribery shut me out of school
Drifting and wandering in a strange land.

I was born with a lie,
Haunted by misfortunes.
Mother told Father a lie out of fear,
"It is a boy."

The revelation of my sex sent him in rage,
Daughter is an unbearable disgrace;
Out he ran in frenzy,
Leaving Mother and me in utter confusion.

I carry a stony burden and ancient guilt,
Splitting the family and wounding Mother's heart.
Who gave me the body of a female?
Who will return my right as a woman?

Haiku

Delivery room,
Shrill cry of an infant girl,
A long black silence.

Elizabeth Mische
Minnesota - USA

All These Deserts

Somewhere in the Sudan
a dark child is dying, and I
am westbound again on I-94,
one hour from home. The sun loiters
on the centerline, just the other side
of Fargo.
Between here and there
my brown-eyed daughters are complaining
about the luxury of cooking:
one girl is cleaning carrots badly,
another watches that the oil
doesn't burn. I am annoyed
that these worn tires turn so slowly,
and expect the smallest girl to forget
to lay out bread and paper napkins.
Mine is the big job:
figuring cartons of milk to last
'til the inevitable payday;
remembering which daughter eats
pork, which torsk, which
only lettuce, avocadoes, and yellow cheese;
I am forever throwing away onions.
By the time I get to Silver Creek
two more dark eyes gaze blank;
at Clearwater, another pair are gone;
by County Road 11 half a dozen witnesses
to dawn on deserts far away from St. Augusta   Rockville
Avon   Albany   Freeport
have gone out of the reach of hunger's teeth
and the grip of abandonment.
I hurry home
to throw my loose change
into a tea-tin marked   imported
genuine; in red crayon   Hungry Kids.
The littlest girl asks,

what kept you? as the sun
slouches into the next hemisphere.

Bengü Gürtuna
TURKEY

Nerede? *(Where?)*

Şu anda ben şarkı söylerken
Kimbilir, nerede, hangi çocuk yalnız.

Şu anda ben yemek yerken
Kimbilir, nerede, hangi çocuk aç.

Şu anda ben çok mutlu iken
Kimbilir, nerede, hangi çocuk sevgiye muhtaç.

Where?
    (English translation by the poet)

While I am singing at the moment,
Who knows, where and which child is lonely.

While I am eating now,
Who knows, where and which child is hungry.

While I am very happy right now,
Who knows, where and which child needs love.

Rosa Bogar
Minnesota - USA

I See Me

I see me in you, little girl
Take hold of this cold world
Don't be persuaded
By his hip talk
His cool walk.
How can he promise
You the world
When he doesn't own
Himself?

Feride Papleka
ALBANIA

Goddesses

You girls carelessly walking,
Untouched by evils of life,
Small goddesses you are.
Your eyes - moons of Jupiter
Your mouths - the rose of Angel Silenus.
Your hands Laurels are, where sleeping is
The nymph loved by Apollon.
Your legs are two bells
Filling with music ways.
But this miserable world
Gives no damn you goddesses are.
Neither gardens on your hairs it can see,
Nor the twelve nightingales and their nest.
It cannot grasp that harmony
Out of your soul comes:
Dawns, change of seasons, gilding.
Love and eternity is given form within you.
From UR town of Abraham
To Zeta town sleeping in cosmic nebula.

Maya Tuewon (age 14)
Minnesota - USA

Through the Window

Stranger staring from behind a glass window
into a world she hardly knows.
In fact, the world frightens her
and angers her.
In many ways, she does not want to step from
behind the glass window.

It tempts her violently.
But she tries with all that is herself to avoid
such a thing.
She wants to stay in God's grace and protection.
But a voice from beyond the window calls to her.
She then turns her back on the window defiantly.
And promises to herself and God that she will
never let herself be drawn to a world that's filled
with pain and hate.
Never!

She loathes most everything in the world,
all the evil that hides there,
waiting to strike all the sad, tear-stained faces,
the eyes that shine with despair and hunger,
the hate that holds housing in everyone's soul.
She hates the fact that a snake destroyed the
beautiful paradise world in the early days.
She weeps inside herself for the way the world
should have been.
And wishes it could still be.

She turns to face the window, realizing she must
enter through it to help.
And be helped.
She looks around the room,
warm and safe,
and then through the window.

Determination burning bright in her eyes,
she pushes one foot after the other

through the window.

Sara Mozayeny (age 14)
Minnesota - USA

An Observation

LIFE is something no one has control of.
There is a time of childhood.
There is a time of adulthood.
LIFE is the time in between.
There is a time when everything goes right.
There is a time when everything goes wrong.
LIFE is the time in between.
There is a time when you are sound asleep.
There is a time when you finally wake up.
LIFE is the time in between.
And, if you don't live a little,
One day when LIFE is over,
You will see that for you,
LIFE had never begun.

Katrina Hollinder
Minnesota - USA

Love

Soft as clouds.
Sweet like ice-cream.
Funny as a clown.
Warm as a smile.
Cuddly like a bear.
Isn't life grand?

Sienne M. Diaz (age 12)
Illinois - USA

Dear Mommy

I love you very much!!!
I want you to be careful, be healthy and don't forget your loving children Sienne, Adrienne, and Dean. We are going to miss you. We will pray for you and wish you much, much luck in whatever you do, since we are not able to accompany you. If you are scared or sad, remember we are always in your heart. Don't worry about us. You are doing the right thing. But remember if you are wrong, God will guide you, and your guardian angels will, too. All of us will miss you very much. Take good care of yourself because you always work, work, work and never eat, eat, eat! (And don't talk to strangers!)
We love you, Mom, even though
we may be clumsy or mean,
but at least we keep clean
sometimes even with Dean
Good Luck!

Sienne
Adrienne
Dean

This letter was written for Josephine Mascarenas Diaz attending the Conference.

The Editors

War and Peace

Joanne Hart
Minnesota - USA

Waking to War

Each dawn is newly strange. We fear
to love each other now.
I no longer recognize your face
contorted close beside me
as you travel out of dream.
Maps are incomplete with legends missing.
Ways we counted on lead us astray.

No one warned us roadside shrines
would be the camouflage
for rifle stacks. Who thought the bread of life
would taste of death? Is nothing
what it seems? The small rain falls
on oily reeds along the river bank
where wind and current work a slow decay.

Dear friend, go with me for a while
and take my hand. Who knows
how long we'll be together or what lies
ahead? We may last decades,
ailing wanderers from home,
old refugees, or palates rotted through,
a net hung up to keep the flies away.

Pj Doyle
Minnesota - USA

On the Home Front

In the spring, when I was 3, I knew no war.
I went to stay with Aunt Bessie
while Mama stooped in fields
to plant corn my father left behind.
I cried at the supper table
until Mama drove through night fog
in the little '36 Ford
to bring me home.

In the summer, when I was 30, I saw war
in the faces of mirrors, sweethearts and mothers
busy at backyard clotheslines.
Shaking fear into wind, they hung out fresh grief,
clipped discontent to a slender thread of prayer.

Autumn came early when I was 39; I was at war
in my own home. My skin blue, my cheeks swollen,
I could not grasp the day firmly enough
to hold off the dusk. Promises taunted me,
their smell so thick, sure fingers
might have cut dresses from them.

Startled by winter this year, I speak out.
War is not confined to alien borders.
Peace is not reserved to idle battlefields.
Fallow folds shrug a gray sky,
leave no shadow upon unpainted snow.
I shed the last icy tears no one sees;
I cannot sing loud enough
to plea that tender fields
be left to a moment of peace
I have wanted for so long.

Erin's Ire

We have to send them back to it.
Children come in summer, displaced into calm
arms and Minnesota lakes. Days of woods and
river swings drown sounds of scalded oaths
and gunfire in old streets.
Sleeping in strange beds frees dreams
to bandage brutal words, ease ancestral rhythms
beating in young veins.
Weeks pass, homesickness fades in the light
of wild berries. Now it is time to send them
back to the clutch of dark questions.
Our only comfort is knowing we have armed them
with peace.

Sheila A. Williams
Minnesota - USA

Another War

From a distance I hear gunshots ring out
I can't help but wonder what it's all about

Another drug deal gone bad? Have people gone mad?
It's really quite sad that no peace can be had

So I keep my drapes drawn very tight
And I'm afraid to look out of my window at night

I hear the squeal of sirens all around
Someone is lying and dying on the ground

It's hard to live in this battlefield
Trying to survive and not get killed

This neighborhood's filled with so much danger
It hurts to see so much pain and anger

Mothers watch over their children and pray
Afraid to let them go ouside to play

Another war I guess you could say
At least to me it seems that way

A war where most of its victims are young
A war that's claimed a daughter or son

A war that makes people too afraid to speak
When crime and violence are witnessed in the street

A war where too much blood has been shed
A war where too many people are dead

A war too difficult to comprehend
Another war, my God, when will it end?

Alma Henry
ENGLAND

The Folly of War

War means death, breeds much hate
    Spills much blood, destroys your mate
War abounds because of selfish greed
    Creates the same results whatever our creed

War causes devastation, leaves many poor
    Brings anguish and pain that hurts to the core
War makes orphans of children, widows of wives
    Leaves millions hungry, with uprooted lives

Men start wars, it is time they were stopped
    Only women can ensure they are totally blocked
We have a beautiful world, let's keep it that way
    Free from war and safe for our children today
        and every day

Pj Doyle
Minnesota - USA

The Singing Bear

A white bear sings peace.
I do not make this up
nor try to shock you.
Peace is the soul of this bear.
She rears back in bright light,
roars harmony
into the sky above.
Her roots are in the cold sea
and the fire of midnight suns.
Sometimes she creeps far out onto a floe,
warms her heart in the calm of life
and so mystifies the solitude
that stars strew color
into the awestruck night.

Beth Peterson
Minnesota - USA

Peace

PEACE is social justice. PEACE is love vision that searches for truth
and sees and speaks and does the truth in every breath, in every
thought, in every action. PEACE is justice. PEACE confronts greed.
PEACE brings invisible to light. PEACE listens. PEACE responds.
PEACE gleams in the eye. PEACE sings. PEACE dances. PEACE
flows in tears of change. PEACE confronts fear. PEACE challenges.
PEACE fights for justice against all odds. PEACE struggles constant-
ly, completely, persistently. PEACE dreams. PEACE soars with the
birds. PEACE transforms like the butterfly. PEACE crawls through
the garbage like the maggot, like the earth worm slowly digesting
garbage into fertile soil - for inception, for struggle, for birth, for
growth, for liberation, for solidarity, for flight. PEACE is justice.
PEACE with justice is life for all - creatures, cultures, earth and sky.
PEACE.

Naima Richmond
Minnesota - USA

Peace When

When we care for our Mothers, Fathers, our Elders
Feed, clothe and shelter each other
Provide equal distribution of goods, the
Right to a job, decent housing, and transportation
Then there will be PEACE! Then there will be PEACE!

When there is respect for another being; one's
Ethnicity, gender, sexual/religious preference
The right to pursue one's own destiny
The right to be human
Then there will be PEACE! Then there will be PEACE!

When the violence against women, children
And each other ceases
Men come together to settle conflict
With each other, accept each other's views
In harmony and study war no more
Then there will be PEACE! Then there will be PEACE!

When there is PEACE in our hearts
Where PEACE gets its start
And it flows through each vein
PEACE will reign.
Then there will be PEACE! Then there will be PEACE!

Mehri Shah Hosseini
IRAN

Equality, Peace, Development *(in Farsi)*

ﺧﺮ ﺷﺮ ﻫﻮﺵ ﻣﺮ ﺩﺭﺷﻮﺯ
ﻣﺮﺵ ﻓﻮﺯﺵ
ﻓﻮﻫﻮﺯ ﻫﻮﺵ
ﻣﺮﺵ ﻫﻮﻥ
ﻓﻮﺭﺵ ﻣﺮﺭ ﻋﻮﻣﺮ
ﻣﺮﻣﺮﻣﻮﻥ
ﻫﻮﻣﺮﺵ ﻣﺮﻣﺮ
ﻓﻮﻣﻮﻣﺮ ﺷﻮﺭﺩ
ﻋﻮﻣﺮﻣﺮﻋﻮ
ﻓﻮﻫﻮﺵ ﻣﺮﺵ
ﻋﻮﺵ ﺵ ﻣﺮﻣﺮ ﺵﺭ
ﻋﻮﺷﺮﺩ
ﻣﺮﻋﻮﺯ
ﻣﺮﻓﻮﻋﻮﺯ ﻣﺮ
ﻓﻮﻫﺮ ﻫﻮﺯ
ﻋﻮ ﻋﻮﻣﺮﻋﻮ ﻫﻮ ﺷﺮ
ﻋﻮﻣﺮﺵ ﻫﻮﺯﺵ
*ﻣﺮﻓﻮﻋﻮﺯ

Equality, Peace, Development
(English translation by the poet)

Put your hands in mine.
Let's cry the song of peace.
    My daughter,
don't let the nightmare of war
destroy your nice dreams.
    Easy on my side,
      with the foot of try
think of the future, making a difference
    the world developed.
    And remember,
        never forget your rights.

Anna B. Rasztabiga
AUSTRALIA

Peace in Hearts

Know that with yourself is a great place
To start.
Hard and difficult it can be to be at
Peace;   to just be.

Move through the difficult days
With open eyes and clarity.
Justify plans to yourself, alone.
Move into clear, comfort zones.

You can't be responsible for
Another's actions.
Care. Be audacious, aware.
The steps to paths
of a greater destiny are there.

Lehn Benjamin
Minnesota - USA

love

take 1 cup of connection
        and 1/2 cup of soul
slowly pour in the colors of the rainbow and stir

in a separate dish mix
        3 Tbs. of justice
        1 tsp. of liberation
        a pinch of passion
        and a dash of revolution

mix ingredients all together and
bake in peace for 30 minutes
let cool

serves the world

Naima Richmond
Minnesota - USA

Love and Peace

Love comes in all sizes
Big, little, short and tall
And that's not all
It is human
Speaks many languages

It comes together sometimes
In the oddest places
A church, picnic, convention or school
Love has no particular place, time or rule

It comes together for various reasons
Loneliness, friendship or kinship
Or hoping for PEACE!

Love, like a river
Goes upstream and downstream
Flowing from me to you
And from you to me

Over hills and valleys
The highways and airways
Love is what we need for unity
Over here and over there
Love and peace be everywhere

June I. Degnan
Alaska - USA

A Warrior of Peace

to face the brutal and hostile world
    without losing hope
to stare into oppression's evil eye
    and never be intimidated
to forge ahead and liberate the mind
    despite the obstacles before you
to reach deep into your soul and
    revel in the gift of life
to look beyond the present and
    see the many possibilities
to plan for the future when
    everyone else has given up
to trust one's intuition and pray for
    peace in the face of disaster
to ride out a storm when you are terrified
    to live each day as if it were the last
to remember the world is our home and
    treat it as such
in doing so each day makes one truly a
    warrior for peace

*(From FROZEN DREAMS AND MELTING NIGHTMARES, Small
Poetry Press, Pleasant Hill, CA. 1995).*

Violence Against Women

Valerie Monear
Minnesota - USA

Outlaw Women

"Outlaw Women"
cried the freaky people
with the tiny crosses
of the tiny savior
who said nothing.
"Outlaw killing"
wailed the righteous saviors
as they bombed the clinic
and blood was shed.
"Outlaw freedom"
yelped the Jesus dogs
as they raped their bitches
left with full wombs.
"Outlaw choices"
preached the holy fathers
to their holy daughters
that breathed their blood
on the cold floor
    gripping a hanger.

Margaret Ponder Lovejoy
Minnesota - USA

bronze woman

sitting there calm and serene
don't you know your belly's been
scooped out?
don't you know that your being is screaming
for what has been taken from you?

bronze woman
still you sit there waiting for what is rightly yours
to be put back

in your serenity, I can hear you
without your head, I can feel your tears
though your hands aren't moving, I can see
your fury

yet still you sit there calm and serene
waiting for what is yours to be put back

Helen Harris
ENGLAND

No Flowers

Dead soldiers lie in the ditches
Heavy on the bloodied earth.
Their empty hands are curled like stillborn babies.
The cameras are tender midwives
Delivering to us their useless fetal grasping -
A miscarriage greeted with pitying flowers.

But no one waits for the formless afterbirth
Whispered by women:
"It was this curled hand held my throat to the barn wall
While that one and that one raped me."
These shapeless words have no attendants.
They lie in the ditches of the mind.

Is it only me who sees the twisted cord
Binding birth to afterbirth,
Wound in rape & battery round women's throats

By the hands of unenlisted peacetime men?
In the strangled silence of peace & war
There are no flowers for women raped.

Kristi A. Nelson-Bestgen
Minnesota - USA

Predator

Who is this beast I thought I knew
who lurks and pants before me.
Predator perched on a limb
drooling for me
your prey.

Dark eyes possessed
ripping my soul
Like a ravishing tiger
you came to devour.
Claws familiar and cold

One savage leap - your paw opens
I stop.
Again you pounce - another paw
I push.

Surprise attack now over
a distant roar is heard.
I limp.
Then wrap my wounded heart.

The rains have come and
washed.
But I still stand
in the jungle
while you remain loose in your cage.

Ann Meredith
New York - USA

Bound

Bound. Bound.
Bound by the knowledge of what you did.
Bound by the fear of what you could do.
Bound by your fear which has now become mine.
Bound. I'm bound.

I'm afraid of the dark.
I'm afraid of my feelings.
I'm addicted to sex.
I'm afraid of money.
I'm dependent on love.
I'm afraid of myself.
Bound. Home bound.

Maybe if I stay home tonight, you won't drink.
Maybe if I stay awake, you won't hurt me.
Maybe if I am this way, you'll do that.
Maybe if I am that way, you'll do this.
Maybe if I...
But the blows come again and again.
Bound. I'm bound.

Afraid to let go.
Compulsive about orgasm.
Afraid to ride the train
            to cross the street.
            to leave my home.
Afraid I will surely die.
Afraid I will disappear into nothingness.

Bound. I'm bound.
I'm bound and determined to change who you are
                to change what you did
                to change who I am.

Bound. I'm bound.

Your hands are grasping my throat.
Your teeth still clench my chest.
Your cruel and spiteful words steal my heart
And your eyes take away my soul.

Bound. I'm bound.

Joan M . Drury
Minnesota - USA

For Julie

1. the knives in your life
      are all slashing through your restless sleep
      the paring knife with which your mother
    cut her finger instead of the orange
    you insisted she peel before you'd eat it
    the point of a switchblade
        tracing the spine of a seventy-year-old woman clutching her purse
        your father waving the carving knife
        lecturing you children before he sliced the Sunday-afternoon-roast
    the flat edge of a blade pressed against a young woman's throat
    less threat than the body poised behind it
      the razor ripping through the wrists of that girl in college
     the dancing-singing knives
    chop-chop-chopping at the Japanese Steak House
     the surgeon's knife
     the surgeon's knife
    you want to scream
     your way out of this nightmare

2. you used to laugh
      say:
            you have to have breasts
            to get breast cancer
      you used to laugh

say:
       you can't miss
       what you've never had
   it's no longer a laughing matter
   you've grown fond
   of these slight protrusions about your rib cage
   the doctor says:
       just a lump
       routine biopsy
   you think of your mother
    with her routine biopsy
   routine mastectomy
    think of your grandmother
   who died
   cancer hangs over all our heads
    like the indifferent swing of the executioner's ax
    threatening to separate us from ourselves
    losing breasts or legs or arms
    as if they were spare parts
   or maybe our heads

3. you dream of your son
    a baby again
      nuzzling your chest   finding no nipples
      he shrieks his hungry disappointment
    waking you
    you dream of your husband
    gone hunting
   he who does not hunt
     now hoping to find a target
     he sobs his grief
    waking you
   everyone is waking you when you need sleep
    you cup your breasts
    with affection   in defiance
    you cup your breasts
   determined not to let them go

4. the nightmare is finally over
    no loss of spare parts or head

the executioner moves into someone else's sleep
at home
  you throw out all your knives
  warn the people you love
  not to demand anything from you
  you're giving nothing away these days

5. you dream of your mother
  whose soft bosom
  is no longer there
  ask her to forgive you
  about the orange peels
  lay your head on your own bosom
  cry and cry
  waking you

Helen Gaebe
Minnesota - USA

A Civilized Ideology

We are so -- civilized.
Our homes vibrate in the night.

We are so -- civilized.
Our meals poison our bodies.

We are so -- civilized.
We have lost the gentle spring rains.

We are so civilized.
Our bodies have forgotten who our mother is.

The laughter, the wellspring, the joy,
The gentle spring rain, the green grass, the sunrise,
The blue sky, the visible moon, the milky babies,
The singing birds, the chattering squirrels.

Money, money, money, more, more, more, bigger, bigger, bigger,
Better, better, better, expand, expand, expand,

Perversions !   Kill in the name of freedom, kill in the name of life,
Kill in the name of love.

Rape, forget who she is, forget who you are.

Don't ever remember, it will make you weep. You will weep your way
to the wood. There you will find your mother.

She is the one you forgot. She is the one you raped. She is the one
you killed.

We are so -- civilized.

Remember, remember.

Bring her back!

As stillness,

The laughter, the wellspring, the joy,
The gentle spring rain, the green grass, the sunrise,
The blue sky, the visible moon, the milky babies,
The singing birds, the chattering squirrels.

As silent wonder walking the earth.

Environment

Paula Mollenhauer
Minnesota - USA

Untitled

My Mother
   is the earth
      she is alive and knowing
      she is beautiful and awesome
      she is gentle and powerful
      she is understanding and steadfast

My Mother the Earth
   is my home
      formed of mountains and valleys
      dressed in trees and flowers
      decorated with rivers and lakes
      shimmering under fields of grain

My Mother the Earth
   is with me
      her voice is in the winds
      her body is lands and oceans
      her heart is the golden sun
      her spirit is the unlimited sky

My Mother the Earth
   cares
      she sustains all life

she provides homes and habitats
she feeds all living creatures
she teaches all to give and to receive

To my Mother the Earth
I show respect
protecting her forests
keeping clean her waters
nurturing her black soil
growing her flowers and grain

To my Mother the Earth
I give my love
rejoicing in her beauty
resting in her arms
listening to her song
understanding her spirit

-paula-

Kathryn Gainey
Minnesota - USA

Amazon River

Amazon River,
Truly a Woman.
Flowing, life-giving
Veins into the jungle.
At your breast
The Kapok suckles.

Amazon River,
Truly a Woman.
Providing and nurturing
Life within and among.
Your wetness welcomes
Those surrounding you.
Amazon River
The rapist lurks.
Slashing your spirit,
Burning and polluting.
His greed for power
Leaves you dirty and empty.

Amazon River,
Truly a woman.
Flowing through time
Unchanged by justice.
Amazon Woman,
Truly a river of life.

Krista Finstad
Minnesota - USA

The Island

My father used to call
it the island, his stories
sounding like a Huck Finn
adventure, steeling canoes
and setting traps for the
wolves that never came,
always searching for a
glimmer of pirate treasure.

All we saw was a lake dying
into a pond, feeling the crush
of the spreading fields,
overflowing with corn. The
white birds we always knew
were singing swans.

The island, once in gramma's
acreage, was sold to feed the
fields, the ever growing family.
The army offering pennies
before taking all the land
they could swindle to nourish
the concrete trail connecting
the blossoming towns that
somehow never came to be.

This same army that sent her sons
to foreign lands to kill and
be killed.

We drive the highway to take our
last look at the farm, overgrown
with tenant neglect. With gramma
gone now, there's no reason to return.

The old lake, now a marshy rest stop,
supplying tapped water to the
weary, seeing only for miles,
the dying of the fields, and
the empty, aching silos.

Elizabeth Mische
Minnesota - USA

In This Garden

1500 feet above Hawaii
a woman is rapelling
toward a rare flower
that is nearly extinct.
It's crazy, the way
some people use up a planet.
The flower (six feet
tall and unpronounceable
on the Anglophone tongue)
is dying out because
some unidentified bug
is dead. The bug is dead
because of some unidentified
poison or land clearance.
The land was cleared
and poisoned to jump-start
an economy, oh, back
in the sixties.

So, because what's good
for (fill in your favorite corporate entity)
is good for America, someone
dangles above a cliff
to initiate sex
between a failing flower
and a Q-tip.
Because the bugs are dead,

a botanist will risk
her life for a flower.
For flora. For vegetation.
Is anybody listening?

Less than a quarter
million brown children
will die before Christ-
mas because of a cheap
war fought over
the fossil juices
of dinosaurs and giant ferns.
I mean, 175,000 people
born to women (like me
only dark and veiled
and calling God by one
of her commoner nicknames)
        that many small folk
will have two clear eyes
and four good limbs apiece
(most of them) wasted
because, one can only think,
there are so many children.

More children than motorcars;
more children than millionaires;
more than soldiers;
more than six-foot flowers
but not so many as insects.
        She is 1500 feet above Hawaii
dangling from a rope, trusting
metal cleats thrust
into an indifferent rocky prominence
and always the threat of gravity
to pollinate rare white flowers.
It takes a week or more, if
the weather cooperates.
Send a film crew
add a couple more days
and about 10,000

dollars.

Not a small thing, her leap
from crag to cairn
attached to the dust
of her birth by a frail
synthetic umbilicus.
One way or another she will return
to the elements of her creation.
From higher above
the jungles are shown
to be burning, the rivers
jellied and disgraced,
the children wandering
from various tenuous shelters
into the tentative morning.

But borders are blurry, where
one place stops and the next
begins is anybody's guess.
The crew is ready, only waiting
for better visiblity to begin
shooting.
From higher up
the world appears to be silent.
It is so quiet
you could hear a petal drop.

Susan Jansen
Minnesota - USA

Spoken Truths

What if a most basic unspoken truth is this:
Earth is at once the paradise and the hell,
and we in turning
weave ourselves in and out of both.
I look to the earth who reflects me,
body and breath aspects
land, water, air, fire.
Amidst ruptures in the land,
garbage in the waters,
poisons in the air,
Earth remains an integral, thriving being,
systems intertwining, sentient,
enfolding me and all who live here
into its heartbeat,
its life essence
healing me, growing me.
And I sense the one who creates,
the energy source, the order,
mirrored in all levels.
This is the magnificence of which
I am
at once
tiny and insignificant, grand and expansive.

Can I, the creation,
and in the flicker, creatrix,
do anything less
than enfold all of creation
into my tiny fleck of paradise.

Race and Ethnicity

Jody Johnson
Minnesota - USA

Racism

Hatred gives form to ignorance
and self-disgust
becoming the knife
that simultaneously
commits genocide and suicide

Luna Macdonald
Montana - USA

Untitled

Slow worm of racism
Hidden under the skin
unknown,
      unseen,
            unfelt
Yet
squirms through fertile core
with hateful barbs.
Crushed
I scream silently
gather strength
from Sisters

arms enfold
again
I face the world.

Hedy Bruyns-Tripp
Minnesota - USA
(originally from Singapore)

What I Am

You ask me -
What I am.

I am Eurasian.

I am not White
Never thought of My Self as White
Never wanted to be White.

Neither am I fully Asian -
Just my great-grandfather
        was Chinese.
Adopted by an Irish family to continue their
        patriarchal line -
McGuire.

I have been seen on the Margins of all Cultures.
Sometimes blending in...
Sometimes standing out.

And what of My Children?
You call them *Serani*, Chinegro and Chewish.
Half-Breed, Half-Caste, Mixed Blood
......Mixed?

Why do You <u>Label</u> Them?

("Serani" is the Malay word for Eurasian)

This Society

I am woman.
From the earth I draw my strength
I am a strong woman
Nine times have I been with child -
Yet only three survived.

Yet I always question -
    Did I have the right to even bring them into
    This society?

A society so wracked with racism:
    That the Asian Honey-gold to rich African chocolate
    Of my children's skin
    Can be the target of hate.

That my black man-child
    Will face the fears that only the
    Black man knows in this society.

A society so ingrained with sexism:
    That my strong-willed daughters
    Will continually batter down the
    Arrogance of Man.

A society so blinded with homophobia
    That my children may feel they have to protect
    Their Friends ...
    Or even Themselves.

This society so full of -isms.

(This poem has been published in <u>Kaleidoscope</u>, the multicultural magazine of St. Cloud State University).

Joan M. Drury
Minnesota - USA

**To a Black Woman
Who Isn't My Sister
But Might Be**

> *"Then we hungry midnight
> birds will have our chance
> to swoop at a morning sky."
> from "The Bird Cage"
> --Paulette Childress White*

glossy-black raven
white-washed seagull
scavengers both
feeding on the scraps
of others' lives
drifting in the shadows
beating our clipped wings
against the midnight sky
pecking our sharp beaks
against closed doors
our dreams
slipping away
like fireflies at dawn

we must feed each other
beg no more
march in the daylight
heal our wounds
spread our wings
and sail into the sunrise together

Sheila A. Williams
Minnesota - USA

Racism's Hate

There are victims
who paid in many ways
who suffer from loss
like the holocaust

Some cried, some died
some were kicked
in their backside

Forced to bend, to defend
because of the melanin in their skin
A bias that is based
on the color of their race

They are abused, oppressed
dying from high blood
pressure and stress

But their spirit
will not be broken
by the emotional exhaust
of carrying the burden
of a very heavy cross

Their wounds are deep
and their pain is great
Why must they still suffer
from this terrible fate
of racism and its
despicable hate

Barbara Kellett
Minnesota - USA

Finding the Great Whatever "Is"

Out of the depths of the human race

Rises a monster in the form of an octopus.

This octopus undulates, squirms, and flows into the ocean of life.

This ocean of life with its vast forms and images,

Its vast diversity and commonality.

This octopus sends its tentacles

Out, over, through and in between

The forms, images, diversity.

Whenever the octopus rises

Its common destructiveness emerges.

The destructiveness of Hatred
                        Discrimination
                        Prejudice
                        Intolerance
                        Disrespect
                        Violence
                        Abuse
                        Shame

Different forms. Different tentacles

ALL--THE--SAME!

Oh, how the octopus flares its darkness,

Spreads its underworld,

Descends us into the hell of Hatred
                                     Discrimination
                                       Prejudice
                                       Intolerance
                                       Disrespect
                                       Violence
                                       Abuse
                                       Shame

Different tentacles. ALL--THE--SAME.

As the tentacles move through the fabric of humanity

They each acquire boxing gloves and begin to aim their punches.

Each tentacle punches toward whatever is not N-O-R-M-A-L.

And what is not normal?

All that is not dominant, of course!

And so the punches strike:

     EXILE people with physical and mental disabilities

     ASSAULT children and women

     HATE gays and lesbians

     SEPARATE minorities or ethnic groups

     EXPLOIT the elderly

     DISMISS blue collar workers

     DOWNGRADE the poor

     MAKE INVISIBLE the homeless

     DISRESPECT "other" religions

and on

and on

and on

and on

and on------

Different tentacles. ALL--THE--SAME.

The heaviness of it all,

The depression of it all,

Oh, the incredible boredom of it all.

THE MONSTER OF OPPRESSION IS THE SAME.

As this monster extends its tentacles through humanity,

How are the arms severed?

How is the oppression oppressed?

Imagine for a moment,

Each of the oppressed groups

   EMPOWERING THEMSELVES

   MOVING TOWARD THEIR OWN WHOLENESS

   CLAIMING THEIR OWN IDENTITY

   ASSERTING THEIR OWN STRENGTH

   GATHERING THEIR OWN FORCES

Imagine for a moment, each of these groups

GROWING IN THEIR VASTNESS,

RAGING AGAINST THE BOXING GLOVES

HALTING THE TENTACLES,

UNITING--WITH--EACH--OTHER--GROUP,

UNITING--WITH--EACH--OTHER--GROUP!

And as they do so the power of the dark tentacles begins to collapse.

The tentacles tangle into a web of confusion,
of self destruction,
of explosion into nothingness.

The power intertwines the tentacles.

The power knots them into suffocating stubs of weakness.

The web folds in on itself and implodes.

THE--WEB--FOLDS--IN--ON--ITSELF--AND--IMPLODES!

And so emerges out of the depths of the human race,

The rise of another form,

The octopus whose tentacles are soft, flowing, gentle.

These tentacles search for LIGHTNESS

EQUALITY

COMMONALITY

COMMUNITY

HARMONY

EACH--GROUP--SUPPORTS--EACH--OTHER--GROUP.

EACH--GROUP--STRENGTHENS--EACH--OTHER--GROUP!

And now the flow is reversed.

What is taught is untaught.

What is terror melts into awareness.

What is fear becomes knowledge.

This octopus' tentacles gently reach into the vastness of humanity with

OPENNESS

TENDERNESS

EMPATHY

LOVE

COMPASSION

To weave a web of sweet interconnections,

To weave a web of solidarity,

To weave a web of knowing that

NORMAL--IS--**WHATEVER**--IS,

NORMAL--IS--WHATEVER--**IS**!

And within this great "IS"

We honor in one another,

The richness of our diversity

Within our common humanity.

A Father Speaks

David A. Lillie
Colorado - USA

A Father's View

I can't ever see the world
Through a woman's eyes
Nor feel the pain
Of her suffering

I cannot push an infant
From my womb
Or know the pleasure
Of her suckling

But I see the world
That has mistreated you
Just for being female
And I grieve in that knowledge

I can plant the seed
Wait and nurture
Sing and pray
For nine months

I can catch the baby
On her first air journey
And place her
On your breast
And together
We can make a world
That she will want
To see

**PART III
GLOBAL VOICES**

INTRODUCTION

We conclude this edition of *Seeing the World Through Women's Eyes* with a section of works by poets whose native language is not English. The poems have their own rhymes and rhythms which cannot be adequately translated, but we are including an English version to communicate a sense of the meaning and intent of the authors.

On the Peace Train and at the NGO Forum the sounds of rapidly spoken words foreign to our ears was a constant challenge to understanding and connection. It is our hope that these contributions will reproduce a touch of that experience for our readers, and, at the same time, point out the underlying human aspirations that can unite us all in joint endeavors.

Jody Johnson
Minnesota - USA

To My International Friends
for Tara and all my other international friends

As I learn more about who you are,
I see more of myself as well -
reflected in your hopes and dreams,
your love for your family,
and your ambitions for the future.
Like a diamond in the sun,
each new insight into your culture
illuminates a facet that is totally unique
yet strangely familiar
setting off echoes in my heart
of similar emotions and needs
common frustrations and joys.
You are a mirror that I look into
to remember the thousands of shades
of who I am and could be.

Untitled

punahapsulakkinen lappalaisukko

luojan keltaisella kairalla

taikoo

taivaalle
raidat revontulista

viskaa

risut
liekehtivään nuotioon

ja herättää

eukkonsa

katsomaan

— kahvikin on valmis

Untitled

(English translation by Marianna Kähkönen)

An old Lapp wearing a red tassle cap
With the Lord's yellow magic wand
    paints
Aurora lights in the sky
    tosses
Kindling
    in the crackling fire
And wakes his "woman"
    to see it
      - even the coffee is prepared.

Angelica Dullinger
GERMANY

Untitled

VERSTEHST DU, WAS DU HÖRST?

DIE AUSSICHT IST NUR EINE AHNUNG

WÜSTE IST NICHT AM FUßE
CHINESISCHER BERGE,
SONDERN KRUSTE TROCKENER HERZEN

PHILOSOPHIEN WACHSEN IN NATIONALEN BÄUCHE
STATT IN INTERNATIONALEN KÖPFEN

GEDANKEN SPIELEN MIT KETTEN
UND LASSEN NICHT LOS, NOCH NICHT,

Untitled
(English translation by Ilse Mortensen)

Do you understand what you hear?
The view is only an idea!
Desert is not to be found at the foot
of Chinese mountains, but in the crust
of dry hearts.

Philosophies grow in national bellies
rather than in international heads.

Thoughts are playing with chains
and won't let go. Not yet.

154 - Seeing the World

Elif Tüzin
TURKEY

A Little Tolerance
(submitted in English)

Being lonely in a huge crowd of people
Eyes are frozen like a stone
Looking for a simple reaction;
Friendship, love or affection
The more close you come
The more awkward you become
Only facing your reflection in the mirror
You look at your own cloudy eyes
Eyes of hopelessness which
Can never meet anybody else's.
The lonely hopeless eyes are dangerous
Ready to vomit anger and malice
The more hopeless the more malicious
No sympathy, no pity for anybody
Just hatred and a bloody heart
You see your own reflection in the mirror
Then realize the sordid truth
You see your own reflection in the mirror
You hate yourself, you hate everybody
Let the hatred die
Let a new tiny seed grow in you
And blossom
Give yourself a little tolerance;
Love yourself!

Aylin Oktar
TURKEY

Summer Moon
(this and poem below submitted in English)

The dance of the fish, the tune of the waves,
The smile of the moon, and the look on your face,
All hint the beginning of lovely summer days.

And here, sitting on a huge rock of glass,
By the sea, on a bright night in late May,
Darling, we both cheer for the coming summer days.

And in future summers, I'll remember always
The dance of the fish, the tune of the waves,
The smile of the moon, and the look on your face.

The End of the Road

A silver dream
Filled my restless nights.
Every now and then,
I used to wake up
To find myself all alone
In the middle of a
Scary silver silence.
And you were so wrapped up
In yourself
That you never could hear me.
But I kept calling out to you
To reach out and touch me.
I held foolishly on to
A silver dream
Which slipped from my hands,
Hitting the ground
(on a cool day in the open air
with the spring wind on my hair)
In a billion silver pieces.

Bengü Gürtuna
TURKEY

Yalnizim *(I Am Lonely)*

Korkmuyorum artık yalnızlıktan
Ürkütmüyor beni bu karanlık geceler
Kendimi buldum düşüncelerimde
Başımı ağrıtmıyor dışardaki sesler.

Sensizlik bana vız geliyor
Artık sevsem de neye yarar
Yalnızlık dostum olmuş
Beynim sensiz de yaşar.

I am Lonely
    (English translation by poet)

I am not afraid of being lonely
These dark nights don't frighten me anymore
I found myself in my thoughts
Don't give any bother outside voice...

I don't care that I don't have you
What use that I love you
Loneliness is my only friend
My mind can live without you.

Leyla Sayar
TURKEY

Barisçi Dünya *(Peaceful World)*

Kavgasız bir dünya
Savaşsız bir dünya
Sevgi dolu gönüller
Barısçı bir dünya
Sevgiden bir sınır
Tekleşmiş bir dünya
Bütüne ermiş
Anlaşmış bir dünya
Mezhepler kaynaşmış
Tarikler anlaşmış
Dinlerse barışmış
Sevgiden bir dünya
Çiçekler yeşermiş
Sevgiye açılmış
Gönüllere artık
Çağrılar yapılmış
Gönüller anlaşmış
Sözler birleşmiş
Sınırlar birleşmiş
Kardeşce bir dünya

Leyla Sayar
TURKEY

Peaceful World
(English translation by Zehra Avsar Keye)

World without fights
World without wars
Hearts full of love
Peaceful world.
Borders made from love
One world
A whole world of understanding
Races blended
Concepts understood
Religions in harmony
World of love.
Green flowers have bloomed with love.
Calls go out to hearts that understand.
Words come together
Borders are joined
World of sisterhood.

Sehnaz Senata Resulgöly
TURKEY

Kocasina Asik Kadin
(The Woman Who Is in Love with Her Husband)

cocugnun elinden tutan kadin.
gözlerine sessiz sessiz bakar

Kocasının arkasından yürüyen kadın.
~~Düşüncesinden~~ , başını öne eğer durur

Kocasına asik kadın
Her zaman, seveçen iyi kalpli
Ve kendine vakit ayıramayan anne,
Gözleriyle anlatmaya çalışır .

Cocuklarını topluma çikarabilmek icin,
Boşuna düşünür durur .
Sonunda , hayal kırıklığına uğrar durur
Poroblemleriyle gezer durur

Sehnaz Senata Resulgöly
TURKEY

The Woman Who Is in Love with Her Husband
(English translation by Zehra Avsar Keye)

The woman who holds her child's hand
Looks with her eyes in silence.
The woman who walks behind her husband
Puts her head down in deep thought.

The woman who is in love with her husband
Always loves with a kind heart.
Mother who never leaves time for herself
Tries to talk with her eyes.

In order to make her children conform to society
She thinks aimlessly -
And, in the end, she is disappointed,
Burdened with her problems.

Aslihan Acar
TURKEY

Dostlarim *(My Friends)*

Öyle büyük bir aileyiz ki biz
Birbirimize kenetlenmeli, birbirimizi sevmeliyiz
Yaşam bazen engel çıkarır önümüze
Hep beraber aşmalıyız engelleri teker teker
Sevmeliyiz herkesi din, dil, ırk ayrımı yapmadan
Bu dünya bizlerin, yaşamalıyız gönlümüzce hep birlikte
Dostuz bizler hepimiz etten kemikten yaratıldık
Belki göz rengimiz, saç şeklimiz farklı ama
Biz bir bütünüz, Türk'ü, Hristiyanı, Musevisi, Yahudisi
Aynı hayatta bir aradayız
Aynı emeller için çalışıyoruz
Varsın din, dilimiz farklı olsun, ama biz hepimiz insanız
Nedir bu öfke birbirimize karşı
Neden haksız yere vuruyoruz, öldürüyoruz
Neden savaşıyoruz! ömür zaten yeterince kısa değil mi?
Dostuz biz kardeşiz, bu dünya yanlızca bizim değil
Bizden sonra gelecek nesilin.
Onlara güzel bir dünya bırakmalıyız
Savaşsız, kinsiz, nefretsiz,
Herkesin dost olduğu.
Haydi el ele verelim henüz geç değil !

Aslihan Acar
TURKEY

My Friends

(English translation by Zehra Avsar Keye)

We are such a big family,
We should hold on to each other,
We should love each other.
Life sometimes presents obstacles to us,
One by one we should overcome the obstacles.
We should love everyone regardless of their religion,
  nationality or race.
This world is ours,
We should live together as our hearts desire.
We are friends.
All of us are made of bone and flesh.
The colors of our eyes or the style of our hair
  may be different
But we are united,
The Turk, the Christian, the Muslim, the Jew,
We are together in the same life
We work for the same goals.
It doesn't matter that our language or our religion
  may be different,
We are all human.
What is this hatred towards each other?
Why do we shoot and kill without right?
Why do we fight?
Isn't life short enough?
We are friends, sisters.
This world isn't only ours.
It belongs to the next generation following us
We should leave them a beautiful world
Without war, grudges, hatred
A world where we are all friends
It is not too late
Let us hold hands.

Zamanai *(Time Has Come)*
    (English translation only by Zaira Utebayeva)

My land was famous for its hunters,
My land was famous for its girls.
But it has lost its former wonders -
Instead of braids there are only curls!
Mercy has vanished as if through the sand
Muddy are the waters of my native land.
        Endless explosions kill and torment
        Generous people on the suffering land.
Why have we poisonous water to drink?!
Land's so exhausted - it's shameful to think!
Why should we tear off ancient ties,
That make successors be noble and wise?!
Ancestors' gravestones have been smashed up,
Old locations wiped off from the map.
Now we feel sorry, we have no fun,
Looking embarrassed at what we've done!
If for these deeds forgives us Allah,
Think of your future, my people - Kazakh!

Solana *(The Wind of the Sun)*
    (submitted in English)

Sun
and woman's soul
I read in your look
remote answers

opaque
sacred

simple
with you night fall arrives
and also my last question

but, I know, I know
that young women are

nervous
attentive
curious

they travel
over the low relief
of a story
that still belongs to them

from that incredible
never ending scene
they return to you

now they know
that pain
is an untransmutable trait

nevertheless
you already know
you very well know
that this decision to smile
is an old habit

among the smoke
the memory
between men
between women
between all of us.

Mevia María Carrazza
ARGENTINA

Untitled

Una mujer
miraba su pequeño jardín
pensó en sus hijos
y lles habló:

Debemos amar esta tierra
con sus ruidos
sus andares apenantes
y sus victorias.
Amarla
como el sol a las ocho
sobre el río
todo rojo
y trabajarla hacia las estrellas.
Amarla
con nuestros muertos
y sus historias incumplídas,
con el sudor del campesino
y la fortaleza de las madres
partiendo cada mañana
de los hijos al pan.
Debemos liberarla
a pesar de los cantos grises.
Ella.Es fruta jugosa,
es pan caliente
y misteriosam ente nuestra.

Es un sol a las ocho sobre el río.
Todo lo demás , hijos mios,
es la siembra.

Mevia María Carrazza
ARGENTINA

Untitled

(English translation by Marilyn M. Cuneo)

A woman
gazed at her small garden
thought about her children
and spoke to them:
>We must love this land
>with its disputes
>its painful adventures
>and its victories.
>Love it
>>like the sun at eight o'clock
>>>over the river
>>>all red
>>and move it towards the stars.
>Love it
>with our dead
>>and their incomplete histories
>>with the sweat of the farmer
>>and the fortitude of the mothers
>>each morning dividing
>>bread among her children.
>>We must liberate it
>>in spite of the gray songs.
>>She. She is juicy fruit,
>>she is warm bread
>>and mysterious being of ours.
>>She is a sun at eight o'clock over the river.
>>All the rest, my children,
>>is the sowing of the seeds.

Mevia María Carrazza
ARGENTINA

La Cita *(The Date)*

Una mujer
caminaba por la calle nocturna
 dejando perfumes dulces

                        por el aire
                    y decía:

"Otra vez
 como todos los días
 una aventura sin sueños
 nacerá de la nada.
 El hombre que me espera ,
 abrirá la puerta ,
 correrá la cortina antigüa ,
 que abriga la casa prohibida ,
 para sentirse oculto
 y se desplomará en mi cuerpo,
 sintiendo que me ama.
 Cuando termine la hora
 se irá lejos.
 Quedaré sola,
 como una fatalidad presentída.
 Por rutina
 acomodaré mis rulos
 y me vestiré
 para estar más desnuda.
 Algún dólar me sonreirá
 por debajo de la almohada
 y nos irémos juntos de paseo
 buscando el oficio.

Mevia María Carrazza
ARGENTINA

The Date

(English translation by Marilyn M. Cuneo)

A woman
walked through the nocturnal street
 leaving sweet perfumes
                    in the air
                     and she said:
Once again
just like every day
a dreamless adventure
will be born from nothing.
The man who waits for me
will open the door,
will close the ancient curtain
that shelters the forbidden house
in order to feel hidden
and he will fall over my body
feeling that he loves me.
When the hour is over
he will go far away.
   I will remain alone
   like a foreboding fatality.
   Routinely
    I will fix my hair
    and I will get dressed
    only to be more naked.
    Some money will smile at me
    from under the pillow
    and we will go for a walk together
    in search of business.

Antonieta Rodríguez París
CHILE

Adjetivos *(Adjectives)*

> " *En la mayor parte de los casos es imposible*
> *dar a conocer por medio de un Sustantivo, sin*
> *el auxilio de otras palabras, aquel objeto par-*
> *ticular en que estamos pensando.* "

ANDRES BELLO

Ni las computadoras están programadas
para cálculos
que el delirio hace complicados.

No quiero repetir las mismas palabras
debe haber alguna Forma Femenina
de llenar las sílabas
que los tecnicismos
han dejado vacías.

Otro Verbo Más. *(One More Verb.)*

Estoy como un reloj caído
en un charco de agua.
No puedo dedicar el tiempo a buscar las raíces
donde sé que se esconden las ciudades encanta-
das.

Tengo que encerrar los conciertos,
y guardar la poesía, el pasado, para mañana.
Hay que comprar leche, pescado y vino.

Estoy como la jirafa metida en una jaula
de canario
no puedo salir a conversar con nadie
de la pintura abstracta
que encuentro en los pañales.

Antonieta Rodríguez París
CHILE

Adjectives
> *(English translation by Marilyn M. Cuneo)*

> *"In most cases it is impossible to
> know from a noun, without the help of
> other words, the particular object
> that we are thinking of."*
> *--Andrés Bello*

Not even computers are programed
to calculate
what delirium complicates.

I don't want to repeat the same words
there must be some Feminine Form
to fill the syllables
that technicisms
have left empty.

One More Verb.
> *(English translation by Marilyn M. Cuneo)*

I am like a watch
fallen into a pool of water.
I can't dedicate the time to search for the roots
where I know enchanted cities are hidden.

I have to seal the concerts,
and guard the poetry, the past, for tomorrow.
One must buy milk, fish and wine.

I am like the giraffe caught in the cage
of a canary
I can't go out to talk to anybody
about the abstract painting
I find in the diapers.

Antonieta Rodríguez París
CHILE

Conjunción *(Conjunction)*

> *" La conjunción sirve para ligar dos o más*
> *palabras o frases análogas que ocupan un*
> *mismo lugar en el razonamiento. "*

ANDRES BELLO.

Tú y yo ocupábamos un mismo lugar
cerca de la vieja estación de ferrocarriles,
Ahora no encuentro una conjunción
apropiada para ligar nuestras líneas separadas
por un guardagujas furtivo.

Ayer y hoy sólo tienen sentido
en una frase gramatical usada
como un ejemplo escrito
en la pizarra de un liceo de provincia.

Tú y yo hicimos un sueño para dos
caminando por las calles de un Santiago triste
y quieto como el mar antes de la tormenta.

Ayer y hoy son las horas que te esperé
frente a la Biblioteca Nacional,
mi viaje a España y tu viaje a Otawa,
la familia que tengo
y tus amores fugaces con estudiantes de Arte.

Ayer y hoy son las horas que puedo esperarte
todavía, en cualquier rincón del Sur.

"Adjetivos," "Otro Verbo Más" y "Conjunción"
POEMAS GRAMATICALES Antonieta Rodríguez París (poesía)
Ediciones Poligono, Puerto Montt, Chile

Antonieta Rodríguez París
CHILE

Conjunctión

(English translation by Marilyn M. Cuneo)

> *"The conjunction serves to link two or more analogous words or phrases that occupy a same place in reasoning."*
> *--Andrés Bello*

You and I occupied a same place
near the old railroad station.
Now I can't find a conjunction
appropriate to link our lines
separated by a furtive switchman.

Yesterday and today only make sense
in a grammatical phrase
used as an example written
on the blackboard of a provincial school.

You and I made a dream for two
walking through the streets of a Santiago
sad and quiet like the sea before a storm.

Yesterday and today are the hours that I waited for you
in front of the National Library,
my trip to Spain and your trip to Ottawa,
the family that I have
and your fleeting loves with students of Art.

Yesterday and today are the hours that I am able to wait for you
still, in whatever corner of the South.

"Adjectives," "One More Verb" and "Conjunction" are from
GRAMMATICAL POEMS by Antonieta Rodríguez París,
Ediciones Poligono, Puerto Montt, Chile

Natalia Mewe-Fernández
NETHERLANDS

Una Cierta Mujer, Una Cierta Tortura
(A Certain Woman, A Certain Torture)

Detrás de todos los escenarios
aparezco segura,
con la dureza de la madera irredenta,
firme como las islas de sangre
que trajinan por las manos
para desolar, arder y acariciar...
Pero tú llegas y arrebatas de cuajo estos oasis
que han surgido en las noches desiertas y del desierto
a golpes de luna y sol.
Y yo te entrego
mis ojos
con su larga memoria,
y te entrego el feto
ya crecido en mis penínsulas de carne,
y te entrego el corazón
donde germina la lengua de la sabiduría comunicativa.
Me arrancarás este secreto
que tú crees que pertenece a los tuyos
y no lo lograrás sino haciendo saltar mi cuerpo en pedazos,
y aún así sentiré el alivio
del Cristo liberado por fin de su corona
de espinas.
Intentarás sacarme información que no poseo,
en ese cuarto oscuro
que está siendo testigo sin entrañas y cuadrangular
de mi carne abierta.
Te llevarás todo y nada,
porque los muertos no hablan,
aunque a veces griten por encima de
los ángulos gigantes de las constelaciones.
Pero después de mi fusilamiento
viene el alba y la luz llenará
de redención espacios donde sólo

Natalia Mewe-Fernández
NETHERLANDS

A Certain Woman, A Certain Torture
(English translation by Marilyn M. Cuneo)

Behind the scenes
I appear sure,
with the hardness of unredeemed wood,
firm as the islands of blood
flowing through hands
to devastate, to burn, to caress...
But you arrive and completely snatch away these oases
that have loomed up on deserted and desert-like nights
struck by blows from the moon and the sun.
And I surrender to you
my eyes
with their long memory,
and I surrender to you the fetus
now grown in my peninsulas of flesh,
and I surrender to you my heart
where the language of communicative wisdom germinates.
You will tear this secret from me
which you believe belongs to you and yours
and you will not succeed except by making my body explode into
    pieces,
and even then I will feel the relief
of Christ finally freed from his crown
of thorns.
You will try to get information from me that I don't possess,
in that dark room which is
heartless and quadrangular witness
of my open flesh.
You will take away all and nothing,
because the dead do not speak,
although at times they may shout above
the giant angles of the constellations.
But after my execution
dawn will come and the light will fill with redemption
the spaces where only

está el silencio. Y mi sangre
se aupará; inflamada, a la memoria de mis hermanos,
y allí voceará la otra mitad
de su secreto. La que tú no pudiste
arrancarme de la boca temblante y
despedazada, la que quedó entre la muerte
y mi cuerpo.

Li Xiayu
Beijing, CHINA

Needle, Thread, and Woman *(in Chinese)*

针连着线,柔弱如丝,坚硬如刺,这是女人的犁和土地,哪怕贫穷得只剩下了一针一线。于是就有了家,有了光亮,有了男人和孩子,有了温暖,有了世界。

漫长而单调,女人一点不烦。她让线缓缓地从心中抽出,让针紧贴着苍老或年轻的指头深入浅出,握得久了,针和线就都暖暖地活了,女人也活了,她用针线诉说多少年来属于女人自己的话,默默的,喃喃的,只有女人的心能够读懂。

针与线,能够使人平静地看世界。我们不是常常看到一个女人倚着大门口一边做针线一边安详地看着身外的车水马龙吗?纷繁忙碌,风云变幻,女人眼里大千世界也不过是一针一线,总要细细地织来补好,拿过来就是了。这就是女人的怀

女人创造了针线,又循着最古老的针线走来……于是就有了母亲,在烛光下絮着密密麻麻的指痕;就有了少女,把线团和嫁衣羞怯地藏在自己的裙下……

从此针线之间总端坐着女人,如日月拱天。五彩的云线,流星的针,女人灿烂如太阳,缠缠绵绵,恩恩怨怨,抽着无尽的心事,缠自己的一生。线连着衣服,

silence is found. And my blood
will be lifted up, afire, at the memory of my brothers and sisters,
and there the other half
of its secret will speak out. The one that you could not
tear out of my slashed and trembling mouth,
the one that remained between death
and my body.

Li Xiayu
Beijing, CHINA

Needle, Thread, and Woman

It was woman that created needle and thread, and then came along
following the most antiquated path of the two..., Then there was mother sewing fingerprints thick into her needlework in the candle light.
Then there was the maid hiding her ball of thread and wedding gown
bashfully under her skirt...

Since then woman has sat erect with needle and thread like the sun
and moon in heaven. The colourful clouds are the thread, and the
falling stars are the needle. And the woman is as brilliant as the sun,
pulling her thread of tender feelings, endless love and hate with a pas-
sionate heart, spinning up a cocoon of her life. Thread is linked with
clothes, and needle is linked with thread; the one pliant like silk, the
other sharp like thorn. These two are the plough and field of woman,
even though poverty leaves nothing else to her. Hence there is home,
light, husband and children, warmth, and the world.

Tedious and monotonous is life, but woman takes it patiently.
Slowly she pulls the thread out of her heart, holding the needle tight
with young or old fingers. In and out she thrusts and pulls. And the
needle and thread, having been held too long, become warm and then
alive; and the woman becomes alive with them. With her needle and
then thread she tells tales that through the years have belonged to
woman only in a low murmuring voice that but the heart of woman
understands.

The needle and thread enables us to view the world in peace.
Don't we often see a woman doing needle work by her door and watch-
ing the comings and goings outside in peace? All the complications

抱，多大多深。女人善修补，
从女娲开始，有了这方心
境，她还能联缀整个宇宙
呢。

　　下一个故事又从针线
开始。游子呢？世界已一去
不回，线缠尽了，女人也老
了，一条线连接着哪一句歌
声哪一件小事哪一段时光，
而一根针，是一个定定的
痛，一个疤痕，一个起点或
终点，正斜斜地插在那块布
上。

李小雨，河北省丰润县人，
已出版诗集《玫瑰谷》等。曾
获全国优秀新诗（集）奖。中
国作家协会会员。

and contentions, all the rise and fall of winds and clouds, everything in the universe is but the work of needle and thread in woman's eyes. What should be done is but to take over and sew and repair. That is the mind of woman, great and deep. Woman is good at repairs. That began from Nu Guo, the goddess that patched up the sky. With that state of mind of hers she is able to sew up the whole universe.

The next story begins anew from needle and thread. Where is the traveller whose coat mother cares and repairs? The world for her is gone for good. Thread is used up, and woman is aged. The thread is linked with certain verse from certain song, certain trifle, or a certain time; and the needle is a lasting pain, an old scar, a beginning or an end, stuck aslant on a rag there.

(From THE WORLD'S 39 FIRST-RATE WOMEN POETS WRITING IN CHINESE, dedicated to the United Nations 4th World Conference on Women, Chengdu Publishing House, 1995).

EPILOGUE

Jody Johnson
Minnesota - USA

Mother Earth/Father Sky Addresses the World

You run from my power--the overwhelming creative energy
that gave you life
trying to define me, capture and change me
to fit the narrow limits of your minds--
open yourselves to me!
Accept me for the ever changing constant
that I am
multi-faceted goddess of love and life
Dance with me!
Celebrate the beauty and balance
of the world I have given birth to,
the ecstactic relationship I offer you in myself
Love me!
My stubborn, insecure children,
stand up and feel your own power
coursing through you like fire
and become one with me,
your own self-awareness expanding
into loving connection with others.
Then we shall all worship as equals--
one being, one hope, one light
until the universe explodes with our joy

Events Which Inspired This Book

Peace Train

August 7-29, 1995: The Peace Train, sponsored by the Women's International League for Peace and Freedom (WILPF), journeyed from Helsinki, Finland to Beijing, China, passing through Russia, Moldova, Ukraine, Romania, Bulgaria, Turkey and Kazakhstan. It carried 232 women (and a few men) from 42 countries to attend the United Nations 4th World Conference on Women (UNWCW) and the parallel Forum of Non-Governmental Organizations (NGO). Twenty women from Minnesota, including the editors of this book, made this historic trip, in part to symbolize the need to cross borders of all kinds to achieve peace. The train made overnight stops in St. Petersburg, Kiev, Bucharest, Sofia, Istanbul, Odessa, and Alma Ata so that the riders could meet with women's groups and learn about the problems they were facing in their lives. Workshops and other activities were held on the train to prepare the participants for the work to be done at the meetings in China.

NGO Forum

August 30-September 8, 1995: Some 30,000 women from all over the world came together at the NGO Forum in Huairou, China to compare and contrast their experiences, to tell about their projects at home, to learn from each other, to find solutions to their problems, to discuss and debate their points of view, to demonstrate for their causes, to protest injustices, to seek equal access to power positions in their societies, to lobby the official delegates at the UNWCW, to come face to face and heart to heart with the conditions of women's lives throughout the world. These NGO's and other groups of women activists put pressure on their governments to carry out the recommendations of the United Nations' conferences and often help them to arrive at their official position on the issues under debate.

World Conference on Women

September 4-15, 1995: Official delegates from 189 nations, appointed by their home governments, met in Beijing, China for the United Nations 4th World Conference on Women. Their task was to approve a document of recommended actions to be taken by governments, non-governmental organizations and other public and private sectors of society, to implement the objectives agreed upon in the pre-conference and conference sessions. The resulting *Platform for Action* contains sections dealing with: Women and Poverty, the Education and Training of Women, Women and Health, Violence Against Women, Women and Armed Conflict, Women and the Economy, Women in Power and Decision-Making, Institutional Mechanisms for the Advancement of Women, Human Rights of Women, Women and the Media, Women and the Environment, and the Girl Child. Although non-binding, this document is a powerful tool to keep pressure on governments to improve the status of women in their societies. It also is a clear indication that the international powers have come to realize that economic gains must go hand in hand with social gains and that by improving the living conditions of women, all society gains--men, children, families, communities, nations.

WOMEN'S
INTERNATIONAL
LEAGUE FOR
PEACE AND
FREEDOM
757 RAYMOND AVE. #213
ST. PAUL, MINNESOTA 55114